ALLERTON PARK INSTITUTE

Number 23

Papers Presented at the Allerton Park Institute

Sponsored by

University of Illinois
Graduate School of Library Science

held

November 13-16, 1977
Allerton House
Monticello, Illinois

Children's Services of Public Libraries

SELMA K. RICHARDSON

editor

University of Illinois
Graduate School of Library Science
Urbana-Champaign, Illinois

Library of Congress Cataloging in Publication Data

Allerton Park Institute, 23d, 1977.
  Children's services of public libraries.

  "Papers presented at the Allerton Park Institute
sponsored by University of Illinois Graduate School
of Library Science, held November 13-16, 1977, Allerton
House, Monticello, Illinois."
  Includes index.
  1. Libraries, Children's — Congresses.
I. Richardson, Selma K. II. Illinois. University at
Urbana-Champaign. Graduate School of Library Science.
III. Title.
Z718.1.A45   027.62'5   78-11503
ISBN 0-87845-049-1

CONTENTS

INTRODUCTION

The Graduate School of Library Science of the University of Illinois sponsors each fall the Allerton Park Institute. The twenty-third institute was held at Allerton Park from Sunday, November 13 through Wednesday, November 16, 1977. The topic selected for this institute is one that had not been treated at previous Allerton institutes and one that had not been addressed recently in an institute format. In the secluded setting of Allerton House, some of the leaders in the field were gathered to focus attention upon the totality that is children's services of public libraries. Viewpoints regarding the present status and future directions of children's services were shared in an attempt to answer the big and reflective questions a profession must retreat to ask itself once in awhile: What are we doing? Why? For whom? How? The sequence of the program and the simple but comprehensive speech titles reflect the intent of the institute to grapple with the major elements of children's services.

The institute was neither a how-to workshop (but pointed out the need to specify cogently the reasoning that underlies the proliferation of activities of children's services) nor a conference about a specific issue, but no issue of immediate concern to the profession was left untouched. The proceedings can serve as a self-assessment of the present status of the field and can be used to identify areas to be improved to strengthen the quality of children's services of public libraries.

Objectives for children's services were stated in 1953 by Harriet G. Long in *Rich the Treasure*[1] and presented again with minor changes in wording in 1964 in *Standards for Children's Services in Public Libraries*.[2] To date these objectives or goals have been neither rescinded nor formally reaffirmed. The goals exist in print; do these same goals permeate the thoughts and actions of those involved with children's services? The success of children's services, Sullivan notes, has resulted in some complacency: "In not having to justify initiation of children's services, we have failed to review and revise the goals which brought that service into existence." Sullivan proposes that goals must be developed by the individual directly concerned with providing services. These goals should evolve from a personal commitment to construct and implement them and should be stated with regard for the entire public of children's services.

Spodek outlines conflicting conceptions of the early childhood curriculum and the child development theories related to these conceptions. The ideological position, or conception of knowledge, which each person or institution supports consciously or unwittingly, determines how provision is made for learning to occur. Spodek draws upon the three thrusts of education identified by Kohlberg and Mayer (romantic, cultural transmission and progressive) to show the child in the setting each creates. Some implications for librarians are mentioned but, appropriately, it is left to each librarian to relate these ideological positions to his/her conceptions of childhood and knowledge. Are the experiences and environments that are provided in keeping with these conceptions or do they present ambiguities?

The responsibilities of the learner in acquiring reading skills and the roles of the effective teacher are explored by Canney. He synthesizes the various approaches to reading instruction and presents a typical lesson plan. The contribution which parents and librarians can make to the difficult task of learning to read, without confusing or duplicating instruction in school, is to instill the motivation to read. Canney urges that "no child, regardless of reading level, should ever be made to feel that a book of his choice is too difficult or too easy for him."

Broderick introduces panelists who describe an ideal children's librarian from their special vantage points. Shaw elaborates on the need for the children's librarian to have knowledge of: (1) the total environment that may affect or be affected by children, (2) children and their world, and (3) the philosophy, organization and program of service that will make service to children an integral part of the total library. Field indicates that in addition to having all the essential qualities of librarians, the children's librarian must have a liking for children as individuals and a keen appreciation of children's books. Chait envisions a person who is intelligent and articulate. Rogers reports a discussion with a group of children who concluded that the children's librarian should understand children and like to work with them, and should be knowledgeable about books. Hektoen analyzes the responses of adults who use children's services to determine the expertise, materials, and services the librarian will need to fulfill their information requirements. Anderson submits that involvement in professional organizations enables the children's librarian to become familiar with the broad issues of librarianship and encourages the person to explore concerns beyond those of the local library.

Presentations at the institute regarding the goals of children's services, the child and the children's librarian preceded the discussion about the services provided to bring together children and books or other media. Miller channels the diverse activities, programs and emphases of children's services into manageable groupings. Lamont describes the small public library and the assistance given by the state library. Kellman portrays the flexibility inherent in a medium-sized public library and enumerates reasons for programs. Rollock comments on the large public library.

Bush postulates that the environment created in a library announces to all what its function is intended to be. Facilities are a reflection of goals. Specific considerations that need to be addressed in designing areas for children are explored. Called into question are a number of prevailing practices.

Kimmel and Carlson probe the purposes for developing collections and the adherent difficulties. Discussions about resource-sharing prompted the participants to pass a resolution calling for the inclusion of materials for children in network planning.

Kingsbury documents the importance of research and reveals the meager record of children's services. Suggestions are made regarding topics needing research and useful methodologies. The roles of practitioners and scholars are defined.

On the last day of the institute, four people viewed the proceedings from their special perspectives. Fowler, a recent library school graduate, shares her experiences and the impact of the institute on her emerging career. Batchelder, a retired leader in the field, alerts the participants to the changes the profession has embraced in ten years. Speaking as a school librarian, Euller highlights some problems common to school and public libraries and suggests some avenues for cooperation. Todd, as a library administrator, cautions that a philosophy of service based on "baubles" is not sound; it is necessary to know one's product, customer and territory.

Goldhor's concluding comments cast the theme that ran through the institute into nine generalizations or guiding principles. He summarizes the successes of children's services and provides ample suggestions for attacking the problems besetting children's services. If, indeed, actions follow, the institute will have more than succeeded in meeting its purposes.

Many faculty members of the Graduate School of Library Science assisted with this institute. Associate professors Walter C. Allen and Cora E. Thomassen served on the planning committee. Herbert Goldhor, Director, provided the impetus for this institute and helped in many ways to develop its program and carry through its intent. Other faculty members chaired sessions and introduced speakers.

Alice Calabrese, Head, Children's Services, Schaumburg Township Public Library, and past president of the Children's Librarians' Section of the Illinois Library Association, presided at a session.

Edward Kalb and Mary Kennedy of the Office of Continuing Education and Public Service handled registrations and local arrangements.

James Ayars, Natalia M. Belting, Rebecca Caudill, and Sidney Rosen, all authors of children's books and living in Champaign-Urbana, graciously consented to appear at the social hours.

Linda Hoffman and Holly Wagner of the Publications Office coordinated the technical editing of the papers and production of this publication.

The speakers are to be commended for the time and effort they contributed to preparing their speeches and for their willingness to be available throughout the institute to lend their thoughts and reactions to the proceedings. The participants are to be commended for their commentary and questions during discussion periods and for making the out-of-session conversations lively and enjoyable.

SELMA K. RICHARDSON
Chairperson

REFERENCES

1. Long, Harriet G. *Rich the Treasure*. Chicago, ALA, 1953, p. 15.
2. Public Library Association. Committee on Standards. Subcommittee on Standards for Children's Service. *Standards for Children's Services in Public Libraries*. Chicago, ALA, 1964, p. 13.

PEGGY A. SULLIVAN
Assistant Commissioner for Extension Services
The Chicago Public Library

Goals of Public Library Services for Children

Some years ago, Lowell Martin wrote an article on cooperation between school and public libraries which he subtitled: "Or, Why Don't We Have Any?" It was not only eye-catching and provocative, but a very reasonable question to ask. A subtitle for this discussion of goals of children's services of public libraries might be: "Are We Sure We Have Any?" However, I would not do that because I believe that when conferees have heard all of the speakers and discussions planned, and when readers later have read all the papers, they will be convinced that, indeed, there are goals. If there were not, we could scarcely now all be so convinced of the importance of children's services that we would be gathered here, and there could not be the strong thread of agreement running through the presentations which, I predict, will be discernible. It is only in individual programs of service to children, perhaps only in the minds of individual librarians, that the question may not be satisfactorily answered. The most painful question is not whether librarianship has goals for public library service to children; it is whether or not each person responsible for providing that service has recognized, measurable, articulated goals for service. I think they do not.

There are several reasons why goals for children's services (and as I use that term throughout, I shall mean children's services in public libraries) are not often discussed. First, no matter how tough the budget crunch, or how minimal or thoughtless the planning of those services, no one ever says, "We are eliminating (or even cutting back) services to children." Instead, one hears, "We have found better delivery systems for service to the whole community," or "We are cutting out the frills," or "We are reducing the number of staff who don't provide direct service." I do not intend to suggest that all such cuts have bad effects on the service actually given to children. A couple of years ago I asked a children's librarian in a public library system about the problems the system had had regarding the reduction of the number and status of children's consultants. She said, "Well, I'm sorry for those people, of course, but now I think I may be better able to get on with what I'm doing." When I asked why, she said, "Because I won't have to spend all my time preparing reports and getting approvals."

The reply of the children's librarian suggests another reason why we do not consider the goals of children's services often enough. For better or worse, children's librarians are so well recognized for their unique interests and abilities that their judgments on what services to children should be are seldom questioned. Because they tend to work in isolation, they seldom experience the cuts and thrusts, wins and losses, and the special joy of frequent discussions with colleagues who share their same interests and backgrounds. By the same token, they may develop an overly reverential deference to the person in their system or library community recognized as the defender or spokesperson for library service to children. Even I have recently been the object of such deference, and only the memory of my own irreverence for Kahlil Gibran (O, speak to us of children's services, O Prophet; O, speak of filmstrips; O, speak of storytelling, O Prophet) has helped me to keep me sane.

Our rich tradition of leadership in public library service to children has developed because of people of courage and vision from earliest history, but we have too often attempted to adopt rather than adapt their vision. With the idea that we have inherited their courage, we have exercised it as intransigence or just bad temper. Ironically, the respect that librarianship for children has always received has generally allowed us to do these things. The conclusion, "But she's the children's librarian," has been used to compensate for the fact that "she" may be crazy, disorganized, unable to open a window or read a budget; and if she should be unable to work effectively with the children in the community, even that can be excused (because the children have changed) — nevertheless, the collective "we" say, "She certainly knows books!"

In a talk about goals, my emphasis on personality may seem misplaced, but I suggest that almost all the recognized goals for children's services have political bases (and politics is people), and have been accepted not just because of the toughness of their proponents, but because of their charm. It is our latter-day interpretation of the dicta of early leaders that has robbed them of their humanity. I worked once with a children's librarian who was an excellent storyteller, and who was even able to hold the interest of preschool children with stories like "The Poppy-Seed Cakes" without so much as a book jacket to distract the children from her oral interpretation. I asked her once why she never used picture books and she replied, "Miss God [her library school professor] said not to." Since she had gone to school at a time when the appropriateness and level of art of picture books for children were not as rich as they are today, there was probably good reason for that dictum, but to hold to it in a later era seems not only questionable but probably not at all what Miss God had in mind. In my own experience, I recall an early supervisor who cautioned me never to touch a child. I obeyed that dictum for a long time, or thought I did. But a day came when I glimpsed myself reflected in the door of the library with my arm around a child as he showed me an illustration from a book he had just borrowed. In a flash (or perhaps in a moment crystallized from a long period of growing awareness), I realized that my gesture was natural for me, as my supervisor's restraint was natural for her. This supervisor might still be shocked, but if she taught me well, her dictum should be satisfied in helping me to make my own decisions and to move, work and think in my own way.

It may be that the guidance and firmness which most of us received in generous abundance from training school teachers (later, library science teachers) and early supervisors have inhibited our decision-making and goal-setting skills. It may even be that the tradition of strong leadership among coordinators and supervisors has further inhibited the development of those skills. However, if that were true, or if those were the only inhibitions, we would be seeing today the setting and implementation of excellent goals for children's services in public libraries, because we have moved away from those strong traditions. The fact is that goals are no clearer than they ever were; they are perhaps even less clearly articulated. The tradition of success and continuity has had its effect: in not having to justify initiation of children's services, we have failed to review and revise the goals which brought that service into existence, and we have arrived at what has been described as a mindless time of doing out of habit what we think is good, dropping what is not popular or relevant, and becoming less expert and experienced in the areas where children's librarians of earlier days made their most significant contributions.

Mindlessness — it is a harsh term for a sick condition, and I cringed when I first heard it applied to children's services today. Nevertheless, it has echoed in my mind as I have had several recent experiences with librarians working with children in public libraries. One I will share: I telephoned one of our branch libraries recently to ask exactly what equipment the children's librarian wanted for a program, why that rental of equipment was necessary, and what the nature of the program was. In the librarian's absence, one of her colleagues informed me coolly that she was a very good children's librarian and that if she said she needed something, she did, and if she planned a program, it would be a good one. Admiring the loyalty but still needing the information, I asked that the children's librarian return my call. When she did, she started out by saying that it certainly had not occurred to her in planning the program that a system like The Chicago Public Library would not have the equipment, and that she should not be blamed for the system's shortcomings. Fair enough; however, she continued by charging that no one in the administration understood what good programming was or how hard people like her worked. Eventually, and I think against her better judgment, she answered my questions and I was able to present enough justification for her request that it could be honored. I found myself thinking again of Frances Clark Sayers's essay, "The Belligerent Profession," in which she praises the intransigence that is vital to innovation and success, and deplores the lackluster air of acceptance which she saw as characteristic of too many librarians.[1] I agree with her, but I do not believe that belligerence must replace tact, reason or competence in order to achieve good results.

While goals have to be personal (in the sense that they should be based on the needs of the people they are intended to serve) and should be developed from the individual commitments and drives of those who will implement them, they are eventually best stated in less personal terms, and need to be measured in some objective ways. Even when formal goals do not exist, the response to questions about why a specific book or series is not in a library collection, or why storytelling is no longer a regular part of the children's library program, cannot be answered satisfactorily by the statement that the children's librarian is competent and therefore should not be questioned.

There are reasons beyond the field of librarianship which have brought us to this time of mindlessness or assurance or fear or assertiveness — or, as Dickens might have seen it, a time of all those things mixed together. Social change is one of them. We always have had and always will have social change, but it has some interesting implications for children's services in public libraries today. Before *outreach* was a word, much less a rallying cry or (later) a cliché, library service reached out to children. Librarians went where the children were — the parks, the schools, the streets, the isolated rural crossroads. And the outreach was warmly and widely directed to children as students, children as the best links to immigrant families, children as participants in culture, children as people. I have never seen a reference in the literature before World War II to the idea that we should provide service to children because they would become future taxpayers, who could some day control our destinies and our library programs.

In the 1960s, when the idea of outreach was in its liveliest phase, the patterns followed were almost identical to the ones which children's librarians had set decades earlier. I remember reading in a library periodical about ways to win the support and discover the needs of people in a poverty area: get in touch with the teachers and the community leaders, invite them to the library by offering some program or exhibit they want, provide coffee even if you have to do it out of your own pocket, and then speak briefly to them, but allow plenty of time for discussion. Listen to them, said the article, and base your library program on what they say they need and want. It was and is good advice, but it was the same advice I had followed, instinctively, more than a decade earlier — and I was certainly not the first to do so. Service to children was indeed the classic success of the American public library, and its goals, as well as its techniques, were the classic means to achieve success, important not for its own sake but because success means accomplishment of purpose.

As outreach programs flourished, however, a new breed of librarian administered them. These librarians worked with children, yet did not think of themselves as children's librarians, and in many instances were philosophically and administratively separated from the mainstream of children's services. With some notable exceptions, persons responsible for service to children remained aloof from the guidance and supervision of these programs; the results were that the outreach librarians rediscovered goals and reinvented techniques for service and that those goals and techniques were seldom identified with the traditional service provided to children. Am I concerned about who should get the credit for all of this? No, I mention it merely because this is one of several examples where service to children was actually provided and usually provided well, but where that aspect of service was never recognized as being under the traditional rubric of children's services. The recognized goals were usually stated so rigidly that outreach programs often reached around them rather than toward them, and did not openly recognize them at all.

Similarly, some aspects of library service to children have customarily been provided by other parts of the library, yet the goals have seldom acknowledged this. Telephone reference service supplied from a general or adult information area, selection and provision of nonprint media, and administration of the necessary services of registration and circulation are often dismissed, as though our goals and services were operative within time and space boundaries. I have always been intrigued to know that there are children's librarians who make no secret of their resentment of the occasional incursions into their rooms or use of their collections by librarians from other areas, but who manage to go off duty blithely leaving those rooms and collections unattended or attended only by formerly unwelcome colleagues. It is a puzzlement.

Another puzzlement is the question of the relationship between public library service to children and schools. Here, too, there is a tradition that is cause for pride. It was children's librarians who first concerned themselves with the provision of library service to schools. Ways of doing so ranged from exhaustive programs of registration and either storytelling or providing book-talks throughout every school in the area, to the packing and sending of boxes of books for classroom use, to developing many strong relationships and programs of service for the teachers who became library stalwarts. The pattern became a little more mixed when school libraries began to develop. While children's librarians were among the first to become school librarians and to enrich those libraries with their traditions, ideals, techniques and goals, the loss has been in what the public library's program of children's service has become in relation to the schools.

No one should expect the relationship (or program of service) with a school which has its own library, however meager or grand, to be the same as that with a school which doesn't. Yet children's librarians have tended to go in one of two directions: either they have accepted a role as outside consultants or kibitzers to the work of the school library personnel, or they have simply ignored it and gone about their business as usual, i.e., their business as it used to be. Instead of seeing themselves and their services in relation to the school and its program of curriculum and instruction, they have too often settled for seeing themselves in relation only to the library program of the school. Examples of this are easy to cite. The perennial headaches of school assignments — from the horrors of fruitless searches for information about the green scapular, to the placation of parents who are more concerned than their children about the need for citations in seven different media when the topic is the Panama Canal crisis — have been handed back to the school librarian, often (but seldom realistically) with the expectation that he or she will see that everything is straightened out. It is not that simple. Somewhere, a continuing link of communication needs to exist between the public library and the administration of the school, and to exist at all levels — branch library to neighborhood school, system to system. Schools are important not because they are sites for other libraries which have goals and programs basically similar to those of the public library, but because they are a place in society where the children whom public libraries are destined to serve receive much of their education.

The problem in regard to schools, as in regard to other aspects of society with which public libraries' children's services must deal, seems to be that when the schools themselves are active in areas which have traditionally been those of the public library, the public library has responded with not dynamism but withdrawal. "There's no need for me to tell stories any more; the kids get them in school," says the children's librarian, adding to sympathetic audiences that the quality of the story or the telling may not be as good — and that is reason enough for dropping a tradition. Thus, children's library programs have focused on day-care centers, nursery schools or camps. It is easier to find a new site than to attract and hold children's interest in the face of competition and distraction. The number of enthusiastic responses to the offerings of service from children's librarians in public libraries is so great and from so many sources — parents, teachers and senior adults, as well as the children themselves — that service to them can be demanding and satisfying enough to cause us to forget that this service may not achieve our goals. Some aspect of the goal-setting process must be concerned with priorities, and priorities must take into account the need to reach as many children as possible to give them an awareness of what libraries are all about. Special services may be devised and offered to children with special needs or those in unusual environments, but the goals should not be set without a clear idea of the need for some broad-based program of information about children's services for the entire public.

The word *information* has become a loaded one for those concerned with library service to children. In this respect, also, we have shrunk back rather than moved forward, as our goals might have us do. Because the provision of information services, data banks, referrals, etc. have tended to make libraries seem lopsidedly but resolutely committed to the presentation of facts rather than the encouragement of pleasure or even the development of culture, we have reacted by eschewing the idea of information as an important product of the public library. As I have said before, I believe the more reasonable approach is to stress that, for children, the provision of pleasure, encouragement of reading, enlargement of vocabulary, and development of a sense of fantasy or even of a sense of humor are informational services which the public library can provide in a unique, nonthreatening environment. We ought to take every opportunity to say this to the information-mongers who need to be reminded that personal development is the most significant kind of information process. Incorporation of this idea into our stated goals would put into perspective the true and natural relationship between library service to children and the great information programs of our day.

No discussion of goals is complete without reference to some means of measuring their accomplishment. Measurement should be kept in mind throughout the entire goal-setting process. Sometimes, this results in choosing goals that can be measured readily, e.g., presenting a set number of programs or achieving some stated amount of circulation or use, but that at least is better than setting a goal which can then be discussed happily and theoretically because there is no reasonable way to measure progress toward it, much less achievement of it. The goals relating to quality are, of course, the more difficult ones to set and to measure. An interesting example is the incorporation of books of minimal quality into library collections with the intent that they will be used as stepping-stones to something better, with no clear idea of how measurement of that development of taste will be accomplished. In the same way, we need cleaner statements of the success or failure of everything that is tried. Our recent history is strewn with abandoned projects which have been dropped by intuition, just as they were too often begun by intuition.

Having goals and measuring progress toward them are essential to the survival of children's services in public libraries. The development of them is not the esoteric or fanciful activity of people who like to play around with ideas or words. Rather, the development should be personal, in the sense that individuals will have to make the commitment and implement the goals, but social in the sense that the goals need to be stated in broad terms considering the audience. As the song says about peace — goals begin with me, but that is only the beginning.

REFERENCE

1. Sayers, Frances Clark. "The Belligerent Profession." In *American Library Philosophy: An Anthology*. Hamden, Conn., Shoe String Press, 1975.

The Child

BERNARD SPODEK
Professor of Early Childhood Education
College of Education
University of Illinois
Urbana-Champaign

Education and Children's Ways of Knowing

I will begin with a disclaimer: I am not a librarian. I cannot provide authoritative information about library services to children, of either a descriptive or prescriptive nature. I am not a child development specialist. I cannot provide authoritative information about the nature of childhood. I cannot nor will I attempt to present the characteristics of the various stages that children achieve at particular age levels, which enable developmental planning of appropriate services for young children.

My field is education; I am an early childhood educator. I am interested in the nature of schools for young children — the purposes that these schools serve, the activities that take place in these schools (often in the name of achieving these purposes), and in the personnel that staff these schools: teachers and others. I am concerned with the interactions that take place among the individuals who are related to these schools — children, teachers and parents — and with what is transmitted and created as a result of those interactions.

I have identified my profession as that of *educator,* and identified the artifacts and activities with which I am concerned as related to *schools.* Nevertheless, education occurs in many places other than schools. Churches educate, as do the armed forces, many corporations, museums and — probably the most potent educational institution of them all — the family. There are even those who say that libraries educate, despite the fact that libraries have often been conceived of as repositories of knowledge. However, accepting (at least tentatively) the proposition that libraries do serve educational purposes, they can be studied as educational institutions by comparing and contrasting them with other educational institutions and examining the educational processes within them.

There are many advantages that libraries have over schools as educational institutions; there are also disadvantages. The library has the advantage (or disadvantage, depending on your point of view) of being an institution that serves a voluntary population. There are no compulsory library attendance laws; persons who enter libraries do so of their own volition, to achieve their own purposes. Furthermore, there are no educational curricula for libraries. Since librarians are not expected to instruct, they are not faulted if children do not learn as a result of library attendance. They are not concerned with "covering" a body of knowledge with all children; they are not evaluated by children's scores on standardized achievement tests. In addition, members of the community will not exhort libraries to go "back to basics."

With these advantages come some disadvantages. Since children are not compelled to attend these institutions, they must somehow be enticed to attend. The community will not support transportation for them; special hours are not set during which all children must be in libraries.

There are undoubtedly other advantages and disadvantages that a library has and a school does not, but the point is that schools and libraries serve a common purpose: to educate children. Thus, there are parallels that enable one institution to learn from the other. An expert in one field of education, such as that concerned with early schooling, might therefore be able to contribute some knowledge to practitioners in another field which could be adapted and made relevant.

I would like to review panoramically a number of issues relating to the education of young children. The first set concerns conflicting conceptions of early childhood curriculum that have been perpetuated throughout the history of early childhood education. The second refers to related thrusts of these conceptions of child development theory. The third involves conceptions of knowledge and how they fit into the educational enterprise. Finally, some inferences will be drawn from these materials which may be useful.

While the process of educating young children is probably as old as the human race, the establishment of schools specifically designed for young children is a relatively recent development. Its 150-year-old history can be characterized by both continuities and discontinuities. Modern ideas have developed and replaced older ideas, but vestiges of the old continue to intrude into modern practices.

The continuities of early childhood education can be seen in the persistent concern of early childhood programs for one of two types of goals for young children. One set of programs has been concerned with the support or stimulation of growth or development. The other set has been concerned with achieving specific learnings. Conceptualization of growth and importance attributed to particular learnings have changed over time and differ from program to program.[1]

HISTORICAL CONCEPTIONS OF CURRICULUM

Four major historical movements can be traced in early childhood education. The earliest conception of a curriculum designed especially for young children can be found in the work of Friedrich Froebel. The program generated by Froebel was an outgrowth of his views on the nature of childhood and the nature of the world. Froebel viewed development as occurring in stages, with later stages of development dependent upon the fulfillment of earlier stages. In the early stages, knowledge was viewed as growing as a result of actions of the child, an idea similar to the "operations" of Piagetian theory. Education was viewed as originating in actions; living, doing and knowing were considered to be connected processes. According to Froebel, insight and knowledge developed concurrently with the creative processes, a concept still held by many contemporary early childhood educators.

To Froebel, the world was a living work and a manifestation of God, containing a universal order that was all-pervading, self-cognizant and everlasting. Man's responsibility was to understand that order and his role within it. Froebel defined the goal of education as an understanding of the unity of man, God and nature. Froebel used the metaphor of the garden to illustrate that an education should follow the nature of the child, but not mold or impose upon it. He outlined a curriculum using symbolic activities, which would allow the child's potential to unfold as he was presented with representations of Froebel's basic conception of the order of the world. Froebel used "gifts" as curriculum materials to illustrate his concern for symbolic learning. The first gift was a set of worsted balls. These symbolized the concept of the unity of God, man and nature. The second gift consisted of a ball, a cube and a cylinder. These symbolized unity, diversity and the mediation of opposites.[2]

The second major conception of childhood education was developed by Maria Montessori. Montessori's view of human development was not unlike that of Froebel's. However, her conception of appropriate educational activities for young children was quite different. For Froebel the symbolic meanings of materials and activities were important; Montessori placed importance on the physical attributes of educational materials and on the skills to be attained from their proper use.

Montessori was concerned with increasing young children's sensitivity to impressions. She wanted them to improve the uses that they made of these sensory impressions through information processing techniques. The skills needed in practical life situations and in basic academic areas were also important. To this end, Montessori provided materials which differed in their visual, auditory, tactile, baric and thermal qualities. Children were taught to discriminate among different intensities or pitches of sounds made by objects enclosed in a box. They were taught to discriminate among different colors, sizes and weights of materials. They learned precise ways to open a door, dust their classroom and pour a glass of water.[3]

While Froebel's program was seen as supportive of development in general, Montessori's program was essentially an instructional one, although the instruction was mostly of an indirect kind. The Montessori directress used a prepared environment, with self-correcting materials. These were offered to children in specific activity sequences, very much like individualized and programmed instruction found in schools today. The goals of each set of activities were clearly spelled out. Specific equipment and activities were developed to aid in the achievement of each set of goals, whether the goals were to learn to discriminate colors, distinguish sizes, wash one's hands, add, or write the letters of the alphabet.

The third historical movement in early childhood education was the creation of the nursery school. This paralleled the fourth movement, the reformation of the kindergarten into the progressive kindergarten program in use today.

The nursery school was developed prior to World War I to serve as an avenue for social reform. While it could not diminish the inequities of British society, the nursery school could at least alleviate some of the consequences of these inequities for urban slum children. The social purposes of the nursery school seem to have been forgotten in its continued development. As they expanded, these schools had to depend on tuition payments from their students to support their own survival. Thus, they became middle-class institutions.

The nursery school, much as the Froebelian kindergarten, was seen as a supporter of development. Activities, however, were viewed less as representative of higher-order relationships among man, God and the universe. Instead, they were intended to be a way of helping children cope with their immediate life situations. An understanding of the world around them was stressed as an important element of education for these children, as was development of the imagination. Nurturing was a concept underlying the educational and social goals of the school. The program contained activities to teach self-caring skills and perceptual discrimination, but these activities were less specific than those of the Montessori program. The focus of the program was on play, expressive activities, and an avoidance of premature imposition.[4]

These emphases were also to be found in the reformed kindergarten. Although a behavioral emphasis undergirded some curriculum constructions of the 1920s, the reformed kindergarten manifested a concern for free play, integrating activities into projects, and providing children with the means for self-expression. This program has been based on assumptions regarding the young child's use of play as a vehicle for learning at this stage of development.[5]

As stated earlier, two basic thrusts in early childhood education have influenced programs of early childhood education to the present. One thrust began with Froebel; the other began with Montessori. Each of these two foundational thrusts occurred independent of (and even predated) the development of the child study movement. The establishment of the movement to study childhood scientifically had a major impact on later curricula, especially those in the nursery school and progressive kindergarten. This movement, currently conceived as child development, continues to provide an important resource for curriculum construction today. The various approaches to child study or child development theory have been used to suggest innovative educational practices and to provide a rationale for existing practices. It is important to note that they did not in any major way change the two thrusts — a concern for growth and a concern for learning — that had already been established in the field.

EARLY EDUCATION AND CHILD DEVELOPMENT

The establishment of the field of child study, which later became the field of child development, paralleled a major shift in the field of psychology. That field changed from its view that human beings might best be studied through introspection or speculation, to a view that human beings might best be studied through direct observation. This was a move in orientation from psychology as a form of philosophy to psychology as a form of empirical science. According to D. Bruce Gardner, four major streams of child study thought can be identified which have contributed to the establishment of contemporary child development theory. These are: the behaviorist stream, the normative-descriptive stream, the field theory stream, and the psychoanalytic stream.[6] Until the mid-1960s the normative-descriptive and psychoanalytic streams probably had the greatest influence on early childhood curriculum development.

Sigmund Freud, whose concern for personality development provided the cornerstone of psychoanalytic theory, viewed the child in his development as moving through a series of psychosexual stages to maturity. Problems arising at any stage of development could lead to a thwarting of the achievement of maturity. Immature acts were controlled in the adult through unconscious mechanisms. The view of Freud and his followers led early childhood specialists to view education as emotional prophylaxis. The nursery school could limit the major frustrations of childhood and provide a means for the catharsis of difficult experience, helping to rid the child of the results of these experiences by playing them out. The teacher was viewed as a supporter of development, i.e., a provider of activities for the expression of emotions, either through dramatic play, crafts or other expressive activities. This role was consistent with the ideas of both Froebel and Freud.

Arnold Gesell and his colleagues are probably the best known of the normative-descriptive child development specialists. This approach to child study was concerned with providing descriptions of the normal processes of development for children. Samples of motor behavior, social behavior, intellectual behavior and language behavior were collected through careful observations. These samples were organized according to the ages of the children observed. The masses of information were then collated into a set of averages and ranges of behavior, organized by age, and used to establish "norms."[7] Using these norms, one could plot the rate of growth for all children. One could also identify the relationship of a single child's development to a total population of children of comparable age, thus characterizing children as slow, average or fast developers.

The conception of the nature of development underlying the normative-descriptive approach was similar to that of Froebel's view of "unfolding." It was believed that while one could nurture or thwart development, in the final analysis, the basis for the total development of the child was predetermined. The role of early education conceived from this point of view was to follow and support rather than influence development. It was felt that only frustration could occur from pushing a child beyond his capability.

During the first half of the twentieth century, most early childhood programs were consistent with a normative-descriptive, or maturationist, point of view. Early childhood education did not identify specific learning tasks as educational goals, and was generally seen as supportive of development. It was not that educationists were unconcerned with the effects of environment on the young child or with what the young child learned; rather, the concern was to provide the best possible set of environmental conditions in support of the child's unfolding development. It was believed that a loosely constructed, supportive educational environment would allow the child to set his own pace and find his own ways toward whatever goals were desirable. Given this point of view, the focus of early education was on providing appropriate experiences and activities for the children. The quality of these activities, rather than the resultant learning outcomes, were the basis for curriculum evaluation.

In a recent article, Kohlberg and Mayer identified three thrusts of education: "romantic," "cultural transmission" and "progressive." Underlying the romantic thrust is a conception of development as a process of unfolding. Education resulting from this thrust is seen as essentially a support for development. The cultural transmission thrust is concerned with transmitting elements of the culture from the older generation to the younger generation. There is little concern for developmental theory within this thrust; however, there is a great deal of concern for how children learn. The third, progressive thrust views development as occurring through an interaction of the individual with his environment, with the individual essentially creating his own development through his actions on his environment.[8]

Using this tripartite view of education, one could conclude that the mainstream of early childhood education during the first six decades of the twentieth century was primarily in the romantic thrust. However, as suggested earlier, elements of the cultural transmission thrust can be found in the "conduct curriculum" of the progressive kindergarten of the 1920s. During this period the focus of early childhood classes was primarily on activities. Many of these were the activities of the original Froebelian curriculum, modified in accordance with research findings or to conform more closely to American predispositions. Such activities included paper-folding and weaving, paper-cutting, picture-drawing, singing and playing games.

The essential belief in the nursery school point of view is the importance of growth. Growth was seen as "development in power and control: control of the body, a growing power to deal with the environment and to understand their relationship to it, with a resulting harmony in functioning."[9] To this end, teachers were to become students of child behavior. They were urged to observe children closely in order to identify the universal impulses and stages of development. What they learned from these observations could be fed back into the curriculum of their classrooms.

NEWER CURRICULUM CONSTRUCTIONS

With the 1960s came a heightened concern for social justice for persons of poor economic circumstances and for members of minority groups. It was believed that, under the proper conditions, all persons could join in the mainstream of an affluent society.

A number of formulations supported the potential impact of preschool programs of compensatory education on disadvantaged children, as children from poor and minority backgrounds were called. There was the formulation of "a hidden curriculum" in middle-class child-rearing practices that was absent in lower-class child-rearing practices. It was suggested that there were different language codes among the advantaged and the disadvantaged. These and other ideas supported the formulation of new preschool programs of compensatory education. Other support for these programs came from developmental research and theory which suggested that intervention in the life of the child would have the greatest long-term effect.

At about this time, the work of Jean Piaget, which had been accumulating for decades, began to receive the attention of American psychologists and educators. Piaget's theories described children's cognitive development as moving through a series of stages. Achievement at later stages of development was considered to be dependent upon successful progress through the earlier stages. The early experiences of the child were seen as having a significant impact on his total intellectual development. This should not, however, suggest that direct instruction was viewed as effective in moving children through these stages. The child had to construct his developing knowledge. In his classic formulation, *Intelligence and Experience,*[10] Hunt brought together a wealth of data from many sources which supported the idea that the experience of the human organism, and especially those experiences in the early childhood period, had a major impact on the developing intellect. The young child's intelligence, he suggested, is not predetermined genetically at birth; rather, it resulted to a great degree from the range of environmental encounters provided him. Bloom's analysis of test data on intelligence, mentioned earlier, suggested that a great deal of the variance in later tests of intelligence could be accounted for by variance in tests before the age of five.[11]

New power was seen in the impact of early experience and hence in the provision of early education. The limits of growth were no longer considered predetermined. An interacting approach to early education, conceiving of education as stimulating rather than supporting development, began to replace the maturationist view as the central thrust of early childhood education. This is what Kohlberg and Mayer have called the "progressive" thrust. In addition, intellectual as well as social, emotional and physical growth were seen as central to early education. Changes took place in psychologists' and educators' views of what areas of growth were important. Changes also occurred in opinion of elements considered important in influencing or determining the ultimate development of the individual. However, the essential concern for enhancing development rather than for achieving specific learning outcomes remained.

Another thrust affecting programs of early education grew out of the laboratory work of behaviorist psychologists. These researchers had been concerned with manipulating the motivational sets of children by modifying behavior through reinforcement. They were also concerned with analyzing complex tasks into simpler components that could be taught separately and later reintegrated, creating complex behaviors through "shaping" and "chaining." The behaviorists developed a technology that could be used to teach specific skills to young children. This work evolved into a set of curriculum proposals for the education of young children consistent with a cultural transmission thrust. Behavioral principles were used as the basis for systematic programs to teach specific skills and performance to all children, including the young and the handicapped.[12]

A host of new curriculum concepts and program models were developed during this period. While each program is unique, most have some essential elements in common so that they can be grouped together into curriculum models.

A number of different schemes have been designed to identify the similarities and differences among curricula. Kohlberg and Mayer suggest that programs differ on the basis of ideologies. Identifying three different ideological positions, they categorize the range of educational programs available. The Educational Products Information Exchange (EPIE) report on early childhood education identifies three views of human development: a behavioral-environmental view, a maturational-nativistic view, and a comprehensive-interactional view.[13] The views of human development presented in the EPIE document are similar to the ideological stands of Kohlberg and Mayer (the behavioral-environmental view paralleling the cultural-transmission ideology, the maturational-nativistic view paralleling the romantic ideology, and the comprehensive-interactional view paralleling the progressive ideology), which might suggest that psychological theories in actuality represent ideological positions.

Conventional wisdom suggests that early childhood programs grow out of child observation. Harriet Johnson, one of the pioneers of the American nursery school movement, suggests that building nursery school programs requires: "an ordered analysis of observed behavior; the outlining of stages and phases in development; and the conception of certain interests and impulses dominant in early childhood. . . . It must also assume a logical relationship between the trends in behavior and the educational process."[14] Interestingly, while Johnson saw nursery school curriculum as following the interests of children, it was not expected that these interests would be followed blindly. Rather, the nursery school teacher, in constructing the curriculum must "know the attitudes, interests, and capacities she believes it desirable to foster, why she considers them important, and by what methods she proposes to further their development among children in her care."[15] Johnson observed young children, as did Froebel and Montessori. The programs that they generated were very different from one another. Were the children they observed so different from one another, or was the difference in what the observers brought with them? How each viewed children seems to have grown out of different conceptions of what was important — values. And it was the difference in values that led to different programs rather than the differences observed in children. Conceptions of child study are a result of ideological positions as much as is early childhood education.

Not only are conceptions of childhood and of school curriculum a result of ideological positions, but the conceptions of knowledge used by schools are also a result of ideological positions. Analysis of the three educational thrusts identified by Kohlberg and Mayer reveals that each position contains within it a different conception of knowledge. The "cultural transmission" thrust views knowledge as essentially the accumulated wisdom of the past organized in such a way that it can be handed down from one generation to another. This conception of knowledge is much like that referred to by Friere when he talks about a "banking" system of education.[16] Teachers and others make deposits of knowledge (often in the form of books, lectures and media presentations) in schools and libraries. Students can then go to these institutions and withdraw this knowledge by reading a book, viewing a film or listening to a presentation. Thus, knowledge is organized into finite elements that can be passed on from one person to another, or from one generation to another.

The "romantic" thrust views the source of knowledge as being within the individual. It may be seen as instinctive or as natural patterns of actions which must be allowed to unfold. From this point of view, what is transmitted is not as important as what is allowed to develop within the child. Talent, intuition and other forms of natural predispositions are the bases of knowledge. Natural contacts within the environment allow the child's knowledge to unfold. Schools educate by increasing the possibility of contacts with the educative environment, but there should be no further intervention.

The "progressive" thrust contains within it a constructivist conception of knowledge. Knowledge neither emerges from within nor is transmitted from without. Rather, knowledge is constructed by each individual through interactions. The child or adult receives information from the outside world through his senses. This information is related to intellectual schemes that the individual has previously constructed. If the information fits easily into those schemes, it is assimilated. If, on the other hand, the information does not fit, then the schemes may have to be modified or even discarded. New schemes would then be constructed to take their place. This is the dual process of "assimilation" and "accommodation" that Piaget talks about.

Each of these conceptions of knowledge has evolved as a result of viewing children in schools. They are each inadequate in referring to all the forms of knowledge that society has created and that children need to know. Even when combined, they leave much to be desired in explaining how knowledge is generated, verified and transmitted in society. Piaget posits several forms of intellectual knowledge only, and others have identified broader realms of knowledge that need to be the basis for school programs.[17] Each of these conceptions of knowledge, however, is consistent with a conception of children and schooling, and has been used to justify an educational point of view.

IMPLICATIONS FOR LIBRARIANS

Libraries are not schools. Thus, what implications could these ideas about schools have for libraries? It seems that before these implications can be identified, certain assumptions need to be clarified. Libraries have been considered here as educational institutions. (One could probably make a case for libraries not serving educational functions; for example, libraries might be considered as recreational institutions.) Libraries, however, should not become more like schools; conceptions of curriculum would be misplaced in libraries. Nevertheless, the ideologies that underlie both curriculum and the institutions which support curriculum — schools — also underlie libraries. Libraries can be designed to support the growth of children, or they can be designed so that particular learnings are achieved by children as a result of library service.

Similarly, libraries can serve a "cultural transmission" thrust, a "romantic" thrust or a "progressive" thrust. The concept of a library as a repository of knowledge can easily be modified to encompass that of transmitter of the knowledge that reposes within it. It would seem that traditional library programs for children reflect such a thrust. Many recent innovations in library service have been designed to serve that thrust more efficiently and effectively.

There are also some library programs that reflect a romantic thrust, especially as the child grows older. As children mature, they make use of secondary sources of knowledge as well as primary contacts with nature. Storytelling and other library services for young children can also be related to the romantic thrust. Bibliotherapy, e.g., the resolution of inner emotional conflicts through contact with characters in a story who have similar conflicts, reflects this thrust.

More difficult and challenging would be the evolution of library services that support a progressive educational thrust. From this point of view, it is not enough to relate the accumulated knowledge of the past, nor is it enough to allow the child to have contact with the content of libraries, however that content is conceived. Children must interact with information and fantasy, i.e., they must do something with what they hear, see and read. They must go beyond the internalization of the external. A constructivist view of knowledge would require that libraries become arenas for action. This action need not (and often should not) be physical. Instead, this action would be primarily mental, both emotional and intellectual. It is difficult to imagine what such a library might look like, or even if such libraries exist. I am not the expert on libraries; librarians are the experts. If such libraries do exist or if they should, it is the responsibility of the professional librarian to identify or create them.

REFERENCES

1. Spodek, Bernard. "Curriculum Construction in Early Childhood Education." *In* _____ and Herbert J. Walberg, eds. *Early Childhood Education: Issues and Insights*. Berkeley, Calif., McCutcheon Publishing Co., 1977, pp. 116-37.

2. Lilly, Irene, comp. *Friedrich Froebel: A Selection from His Writings*. Cambridge, Cambridge University Press, 1967.

3. Montessori, Maria. *The Montessori Method*. New York, Schocken Books, 1964, pp. 119-345.

4. McMillan, Margaret. *The Nursery School*. London, J.M. Dent & Sons, 1919, pp. 83-153.

5. Weber, Evelyn. *The Kindergarten: Its Encounter with Educational Thought in America*. New York, Teachers College Press, 1969, pp. 126-75.

6. Gardner, D. Bruce. *Development in Early Childhood: The Preschool Years*. New York, Harper and Row, 1964.

7. Gesell, Arnold. *First Five Years of Life*. New York, Harper, 1940.

8. Kohlberg, Lawrence, and Mayer, Rochelle. "Development as the Aim of Education," *Harvard Education Review* 42:449-96, Nov. 1972.

9. Johnson, Harriet. *School Begins at Two*. New York, New Republic 1936, p. 67.

10. Hunt, J. McVicker. *Intelligence and Experience*. New York, Ronald Press, 1961.

11. Bloom, Benjamin S. *Stability and Change in Human Characteristics*. New York, John Wiley & Sons, 1964.

12. Bijou, Sidney. *Child Development: The Basic Stage of Early Childhood*. Englewood Cliffs, N.J., Prentice-Hall, Inc., 1976.

13. *Early Childhood Education: How to Select and Evaluate Materials* (Educational Product Report No. 24). New York, Educational Products Information Exchange Institute, 1972.

14. Johnson, op. cit., p. 6.

15. Ibid., p. 7.

16. Friere, Paulo. *Pedagogy of the Oppressed*. Myra B. Ramos, trans. New York, Herder and Herder, 1970.

17. *See, for example,* Phenix, Philip. *Realms of Meaning*. New York, McGraw-Hill, 1964; Hirst, P.H., and Peters, R.S. *The Logic of Education*. London, Routledge & Kegan Paul, 1970; and Habermas, Jurgan. *Knowledge and Human Interests*. Jeremy J. Shapiro, trans. Boston, Beacon Press, 1971.

GEORGE F. CANNEY
Assistant Professor
College of Education
University of Illinois
Urbana-Champaign

Teaching Children About Reading: An Overview

Teaching children to read has been a central focus of our educational system for over 350 years. Despite the variety of subjects treated in school, reading usually has been viewed as the most prominent of "the three R's." Teachers, parents and interested citizens today voice similar concern for reading. Despite efforts to instill in all children the ability to read and the habit of reading, schools are under attack for an apparent decline in student reading achievement. School critics cite poor instruction, cluttered curricula and a loss of teacher professionalism as major factors. School supporters counter with the argument that the range of students who remain in school has increased, causing score averages to decline; however, the average student today is better educated and knows more about his world than his counterpart of fifty years ago.[1] Both groups also note changes in social climate, especially with the family unit, and the advent of television as major contributors to reading problems.

It is not the purpose of this paper to resolve these issues nor to take a position with regard to the quality of reading instruction in today's classrooms. Instead, this paper will describe briefly the roles that teachers and students assume in the acquisition of reading skills, the general instructional approaches to reading, and the ways in which librarians can participate in strengthening children's reading performance.

TEACHER-STUDENT ROLES IN LEARNING TO READ

Learning to read requires learning both the skills necessary to decode print fluently and to think critically about the meaning and significance of the information being conveyed. Schools usually do an adequate job of teaching most students how to decode. Of real concern, however, is the observation that most students are not becoming critical readers who desire to read once external demands (tests, papers, teacher's questions) are lifted. Students' concepts of reading seem to reflect an overemphasis on word-calling strategies and a passive approach to extracting information from text.[2] Consequently, many students do not construct meaning from what they read or evaluate the validity and quality of the ideas conveyed, unless they are specifically directed to do so. This passivity to print may be more destructive to a student's desire and habit to read than uninteresting daily instruction.

Librarians can help provide the models, experiences, atmosphere and encouragement essential to the development in children of an appropriate concept of reading — one that emphasizes the comprehension, evaluation and application of printed information. In order to appreciate the significance of this role, it is helpful to understand the teacher's role and the student's responsibility in learning to read.

The effective teacher strives to teach diagnostically — he or she knows the content and the organization of the reading program and attempts to match the materials with the strengths and needs of each student. Knowing the content or scope of the material requires careful examination of the skills taught at all grade levels, not just at the grade level assigned. Knowing the organization or sequence for teaching the skill aids the teacher in pacing the program appropriately. He or she can also adjust or supplement the curriculum in order to work on student weaknesses in specific reading skill areas.

The effective teacher is familiar with a variety of approaches to reading and can adjust teaching strategies to communicate with the students being instructed. This teacher is continually seeking new ways to capture student interest, to determine better matches between student ability and material difficulty level, and to foster the transfer of skills from reading class to the student's independent reading in the content areas and for recreation.

The teacher is responsible for providing sufficient practice opportunities in reading to effect this transfer of skills. To the degree that the practice activities involve students in thinking about the skills being exercised, so that the *time* spent is *on task* (TOT), the teacher can expect the student's reading performance to improve.

Finally, the effective teacher of reading must be observant. Through formal and informal assessment procedures, data are recorded that document each student's growth in reading. Thus, the teacher can evaluate the skills being taught (scope), the organization of the material (sequence), the effectiveness of the instructional methodology (teaching), and the impact of the practice exercises (TOT) on the student's independent reading.

The student also must be actively involved in learning to read. Regardless of the teacher's skill, it is the student who must attend, question, practice and apply the skills being presented. To become a proficient reader, the student must have many positive experiences with books, both at home and at school. Young children learn to value books and the ability to read through having books read to them, having adult models who read, and being praised for playing with books and talking about the stories they contain. When children learn that reading is enjoyable, important and a skill that they can acquire, they are more likely to profit from early instruction in reading. For such children, attention to the teacher, persistence in the work assigned, and confidence in their ability to learn to read contribute significantly to early and continued success in reading.

In a well-balanced reading program, the student learns not only how to associate speech sounds with print, but also to think about the content of the text prior to, during and subsequent to reading. Such a student comes to recognize that reading is a complex, active, cognitive process. The reader uses past experiences and the knowledge of language to associate speech sounds with graphic stimuli (text), and attempts to bring meaning to and derive meaning from that text. Reading, then, is a constructive language process. The reader must rely on inherited intellectual capacity, fluent decoding skills, and knowledge of the world in order to comprehend the text (see Figure 1).

GENERAL INSTRUCTIONAL APPROACHES TO READING

The development of the most effective instructional approach to reading has been a perennial concern of educators. Although the pendulum has swung several times between whole word and phonics approaches, a majority of the students who have been systematically instructed have learned how to read.

Today, the pendulum appears to be poised somewhere near the center of its course, with most new reading series utilizing a variety of approaches to teaching reading. This eclecticism, or flexibility in approach, seems to hold more promise for reaching a majority of students than rigid

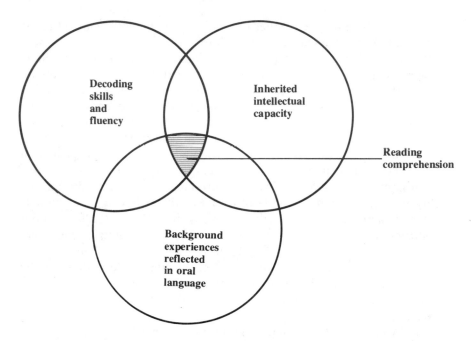

FIGURE 1. CHARACTERISTICS OF THE READER AND READING COMPREHENSION

adherence to a single approach.[3] However, flexibility in teaching requires well-trained teachers capable of adjusting their approaches to the special needs of the students. To the extent that the teacher is not secure in his/her knowledge of reading, the materials can dictate the program and limit its effectiveness.

Various instructional programs for teaching reading usually share similar objectives: to develop fluent decoding ability, to develop independent readers, to develop critical readers, and to develop in readers the desire to read. However, they may employ different approaches to reach these goals. These approaches to teaching reading can be represented along a continuum from synthetic to analytic (see Table 1).

Synthetic approaches stress sound-symbol correspondences (phonics) and the synthesizing of meaningful units out of isolated sounds; analytic approaches emphasize the analysis of familiar words, learned as units, in order to discover sound-symbol relationships. Single-letter phonics approaches use key words, and sometimes key pictures, to teach children sound-letter correspondences. Children first learn to name the letters of the alphabet, and then to associate sounds with those letters. For example, a student might name the letter c, identify the initial sound in the word /cookie/, then recognize and provide the sound /k/ for the letter c; i.e., $c \rightarrow$ /cookie/ $\rightarrow$ /k/.

TABLE 1. General approaches to reading instruction

Synthetic					Analytic
1	2	3	4	5	6

1. *Single-letter phonics approaches.* The emphasis is on learning isolated phoneme-grapheme correspondences, usually through a key word; e.g., *a – / apple / – a /*. Isolated phonemes are blended to form words; control of word pattern enhances the utility of phonics rules.
2. *Family phonics approaches.* These begin like single-letter approaches. However, they quickly identify high-frequency grapheme patterns (*-og, -in, -ake*) which are learned as units. These units form "families" of words; e.g., *-in* family: pin, win, tin, spin, shin.
3. *Linguistic approaches.* These do not isolate phonemes. Rather, children spell the words before saying them. Since phoneme-grapheme correspondences are kept regular, the child intuits those correspondences with repeated exposure. This approach stresses the similarities between spoken and written language — print is speech written down.
4. *Whole word/sight work/basal approach.* A corpus of 50 to 125 words of high utility are taught by sight (as units). Stories are created early and fluent reading is stressed. Later, some phonic and structural analysis relationships may be taught for children who require direct instruction. This is especially true of phonics skills. This approach is the most widely practiced today.
5. *Individualized reading approaches.* Usually reserved for upper elementary levels, this approach has pupils selecting paperback books for reading. Conferences with the teacher are used to monitor progress and for specific skill instruction as needed.
6. *Language experience approach.* Through discussion, group activities and interest centers, children are stimulated to create their own stories. Transcribed by the teacher, the stories are read by the children. This approach emphasizes writing daily. Skill instruction is provided as needed — frequently in small, flexible groupings.

The student is taught four or five high-utility consonants, including some glided consonants like *s, f, m* and one vowel, usually *a;* i.e., *a →* /apple/ → /ă/.

The next step entails learning to blend sounds, in a left-to-right progression, to form single-syllable words that have highly predictable (regular) sound-symbol correspondences, e.g.:

/c/ → /a/ → /t/
/ca/ → /t/
/cat/

Simple stories are written using these single-syllable, phonically regular words; e.g., "Go and get Dad." Students begin reading these stories even as they are introduced to new letters and the sounds they represent. The only words learned as units are those which are of high utility and are either not predictably spelled (e.g., *done, is, to, said*), or introduced earlier than the rules that explain their pronunciation (e.g., *father, helicopter, birthday*).

Family phonics approaches introduce sound-symbol correspondences in a fashion similar to single-letter phonics. However, once high-frequency vowel-consonant patterns are constructed (termed phonogram patterns), "families" of words are generated by substituting initial consonants and keeping the phonogram pattern constant. For example:

the /at/ family

/a/ → /t/ ⇒ /at/

/c/ → /at/ ⇒ /cat/

/b/ → /at/ ⇒ /bat/

/m/ → /at/ ⇒ /mat/

/f/ → /at/ ⇒ /fat/

Here phonograms are learned as units rather than sounded letter by letter. This approach, like the single-letter approach, introduces highly predictable spelling patterns early and minimizes the number of phonically unpredictable words. It is presented as a more expeditious way to introduce new words to young students because it emphasizes pattern regularities in words earlier than in single-letter approaches; e.g., "*Bill* is *at* the *park*."

Slightly to the analytical side of family phonics approaches are linguistic approaches. Bloomfield and Barnhart[4] and Fries[5] proposed that text is speech written down and emphasized the relationships between printed and spoken language. They believed that the young reader has the linguistic competence to discover the relationships between printed and spoken language if he is exposed to predictably spelled words in a consistent fashion.

The linguistic approach requires that the student learn to identify all alphabet letters by name but not by sound. Words are presented that contain letters for which only one sound has been taught. No rules are taught about letter-sound correspondences. Instead, minimal variation among words accentuates pattern regularity (*pin, fin, win, tin*). Through repeated exposure to these predictably spelled patterns, especially in simple sentences, the student will infer the pattern regularities that exist in print. For example: "The fat cat sat on Nat." The student's inference is: *at* → /at/.

The whole word, sight-word, or look-say approach has traditionally been termed the basal approach to teaching reading. After letter names are learned, the student is taught 50-150 high-utility words as units. Interesting stories are composed using these words, with the expectation that the students will be able to read the stories fluently because the words are familiar. Later in the first year, there is some analysis of letter-sound correspondences among familiar words. For example:

l → /l/

as at the beginning of

/lunch/, /ladder/, /lap/

While some attention is given to sound-symbol correspondences and to patterns in words, more attention is paid to use of context cues and memorization to learn new vocabulary. Students are expected to infer phonics information through experiences with text. For example:

Look at Willie run!
See him catch the train.

The individualized approaches to teaching reading employ some or all of the various techniques discussed. Actually, individualized approaches describe more the ways in which students and materials are paired, and the instructional settings for reading, than they do the means by which decoding skills are taught.

In an individualized reading program, each student is assisted in selecting reading materials from a wide range of books. Students read the books on their own, and confer with the teacher on a regular basis. During the conference, the teacher will discuss the book with the student, ask questions about the content, perhaps have the student read aloud for diagnostic purposes, and suggest further readings. Special groups will be created to teach skills to students who need instruction. Usually individualized reading programs are not established in the primary grades, because most of the students lack the reading skills and independence to operate efficiently on their own.

The language experience approach to reading in many ways is in direct opposition to the philosophy of synthetic approaches. The stress is on the student's own experiences and interests and the representation of the language in print. In this orientation, the language experience approach and linguistic approaches share a common view — the text is speech written down.

Students are encouraged to tell stories to the teacher, either individually or in a small group setting. The teacher records the stories in the child's own language, indicating the authorship of each sentence if the story is a group effort. He or she then transcribes it and returns the story to the student(s) for reading and discussion. These experience stories are often bound into small books and form the source of reading vocabulary for each child. An example of such a story which might have developed in a small group of first-grade children is shown below:

Blueboy the Hampster

Mary: Blueboy is a hampster.
Marty: He lives in a cage in our classroom.
Tommy: Blueboy runs around and around in a little wheel.
Susie: Sometimes Blueboy likes to wash his face and fur. He licks himself all over.
Mary: Yesterday Blueboy had two little babies.
Marty: We were surprised!
Frank: We are going to change Blueboy's name.
All: We are going to call Blueboy Bluegirl from now on.

There is an early emphasis on daily writing, especially stories, for which each child's individual word bank proves useful.

From the analysis of student's writings and performance during these story and book sessions, skills instruction is planned for individuals or small groups, as in the individualized approach.

A teacher using the language experience approach may rely on one or more approaches for teaching sound-symbol relationships, including single-letter phonics. The emphasis, however, is on the meaningfulness of text and on helping students to develop an understanding of sound-symbol regularities through reading stories containing words with which they are familiar.

This necessarily brief sketch of the range of approaches to reading instruction has omitted numerous variations that have been tried within each approach. Many other approaches, such as *Words in Color,*[6] Distar,[7] Initial Teaching Alphabet (ITA)[8] and so on[9] have been attempted with little evidence to suggest a clear superiority of one program over another.

Regardless of the approach used to teach students beginning reading skills, if group instruction is a frequent activity the teacher is apt to follow the Directed Reading Activity (DRA), a 9-step instructional plan described in Table 2.

TABLE 2. ORGANIZATIONAL SCHEMES FOR READING

Directed Reading Activity (DRA)	*Directed Reading-Thinking Activity (DR-TA)*
Capture interest and establish background	Capture interest and establish background
*	*
Preteach difficult vocabulary	Preteach difficult vocabulary
*	*
Set clear purposes	Help *student* to set clear purposes
*	*
Read silently	Read silently
*	*
Read aloud	Discuss the story and
*	
Discussion	Reread section of the story aloud to *verify* and *clarify* story content and interpretation
*	*
Skill lesson (optional)	Skill lesson (optional)
*	*
Independent work/teacher assistance	Independent work/teacher assistance
*	*
Enrichment	Enrichment

Source: Stauffer, Russell. *Directing the Reading-Thinking Process.* New York, Harper & Row, 1975.

Stauffer[10] recommended a variation in this scheme, which he described as the Directed Reading-Thinking Activity (DR-TA). The differences between the DRA and DR-TA concern the degree to which the student is involved in setting his own purposes for reading the selection, and the purposes for oral reading in the reading group. Briefly, the teacher ordinarily plans to introduce, develop and conclude reading a story over a 3-day period. This is the time required to prepare the students for reading, to read and discuss the story, and to introduce or review skills.

On the first day the teacher attempts to generate student interest in the selection and, simultaneously, to establish a sufficient background of information to help the students comprehend what is going to be presented. These activities may include showing a film, reading topically-related selections from other books, previewing the assigned story, showing photographs, and holding open discussions. Preteaching difficult vocabulary usually requires the presentation of words in phrases taken from the story. Word meanings are clarified as the students are helped to decode the words using previously learned phonic and structural analysis skills.

On the second day the students are helped to set clear purposes for reading the story. This is usually accomplished by directing the students to examine the story title, to peruse the story itself, and then to suggest questions that might be answered by a more careful reading. The teacher supplies additional questions if the students omit key relationships. Students are next directed to read part, or all, of the story silently in an effort to answer their own questions and other questions that may arise. Under some circumstances, the teacher may read aloud before asking the students to read silently in order to provide strong contextual cues for the students to use when reading on their own. After a prescribed section of the story is read, the students discuss the content and attempt to respond to each others' questions. Discrepant or vague responses require rereading aloud to verify and clarify story content. Further reading aloud may be desirable either for diagnostic purposes or because the material lends itself to oral interpretation.

On the third day a lesson on reading skills may be planned, including instruction for students requiring special assistance from the teacher. Enrichment activities are often planned as a followup to the story (e.g., plays, puppet shows, art projects, independent research or further reading).

During the DRA and DR-TA, students are often assigned additional work to reinforce basic reading and writing skills. Often these activities are found in the workbook accompanying the basal reader. To the degree that the teacher utilizes these seatwork exercises sparingly, selectively and with attention to the individual needs of students, these activities can be an effective means to bolster students' reading skills.

LIBRARIANS AND CHILDREN LEARNING TO READ

After this necessarily condensed overview of reading instruction, it may be helpful to focus on how the librarian can contribute to children's growth in reading performance. The major assertion of this paper is that students should know what reading is, have a desire to learn to read, and be taught effectively by well-trained teachers if they are to become effective, practicing readers. These variables, however, obviously reflect an ideal condition that does not exist for a significant proportion of our children. This fact is borne out by the numbers of students who have failed to learn to decode effectively in classrooms where other students have easily learned to decode. Some students seem able to decode well when asked to do so, but comprehend little of what they read. Perhaps less obvious, but no less serious, is the number of students who answer the teacher's questions and pass the tests, but who seldom *think* when they read. They seem passive, uncritical and bored with the material they are asked to read — they seem devoid of the desire to read. This is reflected in the number of adults who choose not to read once they leave school and the consequent absence of adult modeling behavior for reading.

How is it possible that the importance placed throughout the school years on becoming an effective reader can be so quickly and complacently set aside? Somehow, teachers and adults are failing to instill in youth the motivation to read. Here, perhaps more than in any other way, parents and librarians can affect children's reading performance without confusing or duplicating the instruction provided in the school.

The library contains books which are often viewed by the child as different from the basal reader used in schools. Libraries can be explored, revisited and enjoyed without the restrictions imposed by well-intentioned teachers, i.e., that books must be read thoroughly, on schedule and without error. Schools often make it too difficult to exercise the freedom to explore books on one's own, equating reading with top scholarship, obedience, grade-level performance or work completed on time. Libraries need not and should not put such restrictions between children and books.

Keeping in mind that the young child must value books to become a proficient, lifelong reader, librarians can create an atmosphere which beckons children to books rather than one that confronts them with the printed word. No child, regardless of reading level, should ever be made to feel that a book of his choice is too difficult or too easy for him. The child should be allowed to select on the basis of his own interests and of perhaps some alternatives offered by the librarian. After all, the child's reasons for selecting the book may have little, if anything, to do with the book's readability.

Librarians have the opportunity to provide book-related experiences for children which schools often omit or deemphasize:

1. the freedom to be an individual reading a book of one's own choice, rather than an assigned basal reader;
2. the chance to explore topics of personal interest — rather than being faced with the task of selecting a book from a library limited in titles by lists that dictate what 9-year-old girls like to read;
3. the opportunity to select a book that is "too easy" because of wanting to be reassured that one does know something — despite the bad day in reading "that book that's too hard";
4. the experience of taking a book that has been read before and enjoyed because it feels good to know that this book is "yours";
5. the license to choose a book that is difficult because it has one intriguing picture that stimulates the imagination;
6. the power to ask for advice about books to read that might be fun, but to know that one need not be compelled to accept that advice; and
7. the experience of being treated like other students — as an intelligent, responsible, significant individual capable of making decisions.

Experiences like these may help students who have difficulty learning to read to persist until they not only learn how to read, but also discover the value of reading.

The four objectives of school reading programs should be recalled here: decoding skills, comprehension, enjoyment and desire to read. For many reasons, schools have tended to emphasize the first objective, wonder about the second, and all but ignore the latter two goals. The result has been that few people read critically; most people do not read at all. Since many parents have assigned to schools the total responsibility for teaching their children how to read, perhaps librarians can share more directly and consciously in the experience of helping children to discover the value and joy of reading.

REFERENCES

1. Tuinman, Jaap, et al. "Reading Achievement in the United States: Then and Now," *Journal of Reading* 19:455-63, March 1976.

2. Johns, Jerry L., and Ellis, DiAnn W. "Reading: Children Tell It Like It Is," *Reading World* 16:115-28, Dec. 1976.

3. Dechant, Emerald. "Why an Eclectic Approach in Reading Instruction?" *In* J. Allen Figurel, ed. *Vistas in Reading* (Proceedings of the Eleventh Annual Convention, International Reading Association). Newark, Del., IRA, 1967, vol. 11, pt. 1, pp. 28-31.

4. Bloomfield, Leonard, and Barnhart, Clarence. *Let's Read; A Linguistic Approach.* Detroit, Mich., Wayne State University Press, 1961.

5. Fries, Charles. *Linguistics and Reading.* New York, Holt, Rinehart & Winston, 1963.

6. Gattegno, Caleb. *Words in Color.* Chicago, Learning Materials, 1962.

7. *See* Bereiter, Carl, and Engelmann, Siegfried. *Teaching Disadvantaged Children in the Preschool.* Englewood Cliffs, N.J., Prentice-Hall, 1966.

8. Downing, John. "How I.T.A. Began," *Elementary English* 44:40-46, Jan. 1967.

9. For a more complete description of reading progams, *see* Aukerman, Robert. *Approaches to Beginning Reading.* New York, J. Wiley, 1971.

10. Stauffer, Russell. *Directing the Reading-Thinking Process.* New York, Harper & Row, 1975.

The Children's Librarian

DOROTHY M. BRODERICK
Editor-in-Chief
Voice of Youth Advocates
New Brunswick, New Jersey

Some people see a continuing emphasis on examining "the image" of the children's librarian as an exercise in navel-gazing. There is, of course, an element of this in the process, but the importance of understanding how others perceive us is vital to our success. If we are viewed only as partially developed adults who work with children because of an inability to work with other age groups, our effectiveness is limited. The six papers that follow describe the "ideal" children's librarian as seen through the eyes of a variety of people. An analysis of the papers, coupled with comments following their presentations and recurring throughout the rest of the institute, provides an amazing consensus.

Whether seen through the eyes of a library administrator or through the eyes of the children we serve, children's librarians must possess a large number of characteristics that, when examined critically, define the mature adult. The children's librarian must respect people, regardless of their age; have an understanding of the world in which she or he functions; and possess a sense of humor and perspective. In professional terms, the children's librarian must understand the political processes by which public institutions achieve their goals and build support within the community. Librarians must be familiar with the materials they use and with the children and adults with whom they work. They must excel at bringing the materials and people together.

No one at the institute could or did argue with these characteristics. But it eventually became obvious that opinions of the participants were divided in one area: Are children's librarians to protect the young, to shield them from ideas and attitudes deemed inappropriate, or are they to provide free access to all materials and trust the children to decide for themselves what is appropriate to their needs and what is not? The differences of opinion on this question remain the great unresolved dilemma of children's librarianship.

SPENCER G. SHAW
Professor
School of Librarianship
University of Washington
Seattle, Washington

The Children's Librarian as Viewed by Library School Educators

The triad is a combination of a group of elements that may be studied by scholars in different disciplines. A scientist may probe the secrets which are contained within its chemical compounds; a musician may extricate from it different tonal chords. Aspiring to be neither scientist nor musician, I shall utilize this unique configuration in the context of our concerns at this institute.

As an educator in the field of librarianship, I perceive the individual who engages in library service for children as a 3-dimensional configuration. Within the framework of a triad, it will be necessary to focus attention on three closely related elements that will influence the structuring of any profile of a children's librarian. These three elements are: (1) to have knowledge of the total environment that may affect children or be affected by children, (2) to have a knowledge of children with their singular commonalities and disparities and of their world with its dichotomous patterns, and (3) to have a knowledge of the philosophy, organization and program of service that will make library service to children an integral part of the total structure of the public library.

Our first concern is to have a knowledge of the total community that may affect children or be affected by children. Within the last two decades, children and adults have been confronted with a staggering array of complex sociological, technological and educational trends that have influenced societal changes. In the sphere of sociological trends, consider the impact on children who are directly affected by alternative family lifestyles, e.g., reverse roles of husbands and wives in parenting, mothers joining the labor force outside the home, domiciles headed by a single parent or by single men and women, homes split by increasing divorce rates or by separation of the parents. Probe the plight of children in poverty-level families who are inheritors of a welfare existence or of programs providing aid to families with dependent children. Understand the positive and negative potentials for children who reside in foster homes or who are adopted. Recognize the altered patterns of relationships for children in a growing number of smaller families or in families where there is a breakdown in communication between and among family members.

As the child's environment expands into the community, relate to the traumatic feelings of rootlessness that children may experience with the greater mobility of families. What are their inner sensations as they migrate from rural to urban areas or from one school district to another within the same city? Recognize their struggle to gain an entrance into a pluralistic society with the demise of traditional demographic patterns of community living based on economics, ethnicity or class distinctions. Identify with children as they test emerging beliefs in accepting the concept of cultural pluralism as a needed replacement for assimilation. In their exploration of such a premise, they may encounter tension and conflict caused by adult adherence to worn-out prejudices.

Sociological trends have given birth to conflicts in moral values, unrest and rebellion among the young. Sense the confusion of children as they seek to understand the adult attitudinal changes regarding morality, social and sexual relationships, and aesthetic values. Children value what adults value, accept what adults accept, discard what adults discard. In this respect it may be wise to refer to the thoughts of John W. Gardner:

> We can make great progress in improving the functioning of our society and still not have anything that will live or last unless we concern ourselves with the values that underlie the enterprise. If a society believes in nothing, if it does not generate in its members a sense of moral purpose, there is no possibility that it can develop the high level of motivation essential to renewal.[1]

Societal changes have also been influenced by technological and scientific trends that have far-reaching implications for children and adults. Ponder the limitless challenges for children as they converge upon new frontiers so different from those of our generation and those of their grandparents'. Technologically, during the past several decades, the final stages of the Industrial Revolution have given way to the nuclear age and now to the age of space. Born into this revolutionary era, children have been surfeited with a plethora of technological devices that have dramatically altered the structure of inquiry and the communication processes. Overwhelming to many of us, we watch as children accept with a sophisticated assurance television, stereo, radio, CBs, satellite communication modules, computers, data banks, audiotapes, films and videotapes.

Knowledgeable beyond their years, children learn at an early age to master the varying combinations of these incomparable assemblages of interlocking multimedia sensory components. With a casual flick of a dial or the pressing of a remote control, children communicate with the far-distant operator of a similar machine and converse in a jargon understandable only to the two. Via satellites they may hear and view their counterparts in areas devastated by war or by natural catastrophes. Children gambol with their friends on "Sesame Street" or hear a taped telephonic story emanating from a library's Dial-A-Story service. Truly, the children's hour of today has little resemblance to the poetic depiction of the event by Henry Wadsworth Longfellow.

Confronted with such scientific advances, children amy adjust more easily than their traditionally-conditioned adults. For these young explorers, the psychological and intellectual barriers dexcribed in Toffler's *Future Shock*[2] will not be insurmountable. With proper guidance children may learn how to extract from the media and utilize those messages that will enable them to create meaningful visual and auditory self-expressions. As the forms, functions and versatility of media undergo constant changes, children may be the catalytic agents to test every new advance. Through their sense of wonder and their curiosity regarding these technological marvels, children may be the channels through which new ways may be devised and studied to retrieve, assimilate and disseminate knowledge. They will be the least afraid to try, to err or to succeed.

Extending themselves beyond learning cognitive skills with the aid of these tools, children may find within these same scientific components the means to satisfy their aesthetic needs as the affective domain is nurtured. When the young have such experiences, they will feel a spiritual kinship with the space-searching Columbus who exclaimed in E.G. Valens's *Cybernaut, a Space Poem:*

> . . .
> I
> The new Columbus
> . . .
> Single handed I
> Have pushed to the limits
> Of the veriest unknown
>> The last
>> The limitless
>> The final unexplored frontier....[3]

Conversely, if improper guidance is offered in the use of these technological marvels, children may become victims of subtle, subliminal methods of negative persuasion. Duped into believing false assumptions, they may be morally and intellectually impaired. Their perceptions and values which relate to the known and the unknown environments of which they are a part will be marred. The ultimate result will be the creation of a body of young, joyless strangers. Like programmed robots, they will be denied a freedom of the intellect; they will suffer an atrophy of sense and spirit.

Trends in education for the 1970s have entered into new stages, prompted by societal changes and technological advancements. No longer is the human endeavor confined to the limitations of earth. Man has been projected into outer space; he has soared beyond the gravitational pull of our planet into the fathomless regions of the heavens to the landing of a fragile craft upon the moon. Yet, while scientists have it within their power to send rocketry great distances into the celestial spheres, our educational endeavors have not enlightened the intellect as to how to eradicate slums, terminate wars or grant deprived children and adults a rightful place in society.

In this past decade we have come to question educational practices that have failed to reduce racial and class inequalities. Children of the "have-not" segments of our society still enter programs of learning with inappropriate content concealed by euphemistic labels. Still they emerge uneducated, underachieved, unenlightened. However, the 1970s has witnessed a unique phenomenon: these estranged recipients are demanding equal educational opportunities and are causing institutions of learning to reassess their philosophies, their programs and their methodologies. Simultaneously, as these children of ethnic minority and low-income groups seek entrance into this mainstream of learning, some of their peers in the middle-class segments of our population consider such moves as threats to their own educational pursuits. In the tension-ridden atmosphere which evolves in such situations, antagonism occasionally erupts in confrontations; for example, legal maneuvers are instigated by parents to protect outmoded interpretations of law with cries of "reverse discrimination."

The educational trends have also caused the pendulum, now, to swing back in an effort to still the clamor for "basics." Fearing the consequences to their children who are unable to read, spell, speak in coherent sentences, and master the principles of mathematics, agitated parents are holding the schools accountable. In varying degrees of nostalgic remembrances, concerned adults are demanding a complete revamping of the curricula to eliminate what they consider to be "frills." No less concerned are the proponents of the arts, who feel that a precipitous elimination of other subjects without a careful review will be detrimental to the total education of children. Nyquist realized this fact when he stressed this need in "Humanities and Arts in Elementary and Secondary Education; Towards a New Humanistic Emphasis in Our Schools."[4] In a syndicated newspaper column, the noted scholar, Norman Cousins, reflected on this topic in "The Arts Are No Less Basic."[5] Charles Silberman echoed similar sentiments in his provocative book *Crisis in the Classroom:* "The false dichotomy between the 'cognitive' and the 'affective' domain — can only cripple the development of thought and feeling. If this be so, then poetry, music, painting, dance, and the other arts are not frills to be indulged in if time is left over from the real business of education; they *are* the business of education."[6]

Overshadowed by these societal and educational concerns is the equally impressive challenge to help children in their search for knowledge. It is essential to know this youthful public who attend schools daily. According to National Center for Education Statistics data, enrollment in public and nonpublic schools for kindergarten through eighth grade was 34 million in 1974-75.[7] From the Bureau of the Census, the total enrollment of children in public and private nursery shcools in autumn 1975 was 1,748,000.[8] In statistics issued by the Office of Education, the total enrollment of exceptional children in special education programs for 1973-74 was 3,158,000.[9]

Some of the educational trends that are shaping the learning environment for these children should be noted. These include the development of early childhood educational programs such as nursery schools, day care centers and Head Start. The rise of alternative schools, street academies and contact schools have entered the scene. New forms of technology permit the packaging of education in new ways in terms of length, content and location of courses. It also provides for the use of television sets with self-instructing cartridges, while computer-assisted instruction through decentralized terminals makes possible independent study at home.

Educators are also focusing their attention on learners with special needs and bilingual education for ethnic minorities. Through federal, state and local governments, grants and programs are made possible to extend educational opportunities for all citizens, children and adults. Most important for those who serve children are the educational theories advanced by such leaders as James S. Coleman, Clark Kerr and James E. Allen, Jr., who espouse the concept of extending education beyond the formal institutions of learning. As summarized by Allen:

> We must recognize that to consider education solely in terms of formal institutions is to hold a narrow and unrealistic concept of the

process of learning. Education comes as much or more from outside the schools as within and we must begin to try to shape the entire environment of life so that its influence is positive and reinforcing with respect to the total development of all human beings.[10]

Our second major concern in the configuration of the triad is to have a knowledge of children with their singular commonalities and disparities and of their world with its dichotomous patterns. According to the Bureau of the Census, the U.S. population of children to age 14 totaled 53,649,000 in 1975. Included in this figure were 15,896,000 girls and boys under the age of 5 years; 17,335,000 children between the ages of 5 and 9; and 20,418,000 between the ages of 10 and 14.[11]

However, children are more than statistics. What do we know about the children with whom we interact? Do we know the environments from which they have come? Have we visited their communities? Have we entered the housing developments or apartments in which they live? Have we traveled the rural roads to reach those in isolated areas or on ranches or reservations? Have we mingled in environments where English is a second language and faced the task of communicating with children in ways foreign to us? Can we appreciate the cultural and ethnic differences among children? Can we understand and accept their value systems, which may be different from ours? Do we know them as individuals with unique personalities, human beings with potential? Or do we take the easy way out and put the children into neat categories, referring to them with adjectives of ghetto, welfare, slum, middle-class, culturally advantaged, problem, suburban, culturally deprived, black, white, Chicano, Appalachian poor white, handicapped, native American, etc.? Labeling any individual has harmful effects, and when adults engage in such tactics in speaking to and about children, the damage is irreparable. We are in danger of imposing ourselves negatively on segments of society who are least able to defend themselves — children.

Those of us who are fortunate enough to work with children and to include them within our circle of friends know the intangible gifts which they bestow upon us — the ready smile, the joyous greeting, the spontaneous response, the mischievous pranks done without malice, the innocent trust, the quiet moments of companionable silence. We come to know children through their thank-you letters, their almost-illegible scrawls of newly invented spellings of words, their creative poetry or artistic expressions. We share their concerns in *Miracles: Poems by Children of the English-Speaking World,* collected by Richard Lewis.[12] We react to their feelings as voiced in the book *Here I Am: An Anthology of Poems Written by Young People in Some of America's Minority Groups,* edited by Virginia O. Baron.[13] We walk the streets and experience sights and smells with children as they ask *What Is a City: Young People Reply,* compiled by Dianne Farrell and Ruth M. Hayes.[14]

Perhaps the essence of the world of childhood has seldom been expressed more sensitively than in the perceptive insights of Jean Karl as recorded in her book, *Childhood to Childhood:*

> Childhood is not a time of innocence, it is not a time of unmitigated pleasure, it is not a time of easy joys and carefree days. It is so only in the nostalgia of adults. Childhood is a time of difficult inquiry, of trying discovery, of hard quests and unfulfilled desires. It is a time of bumping into limits that seem to have no reason, of enduring meaningless ceremonies, and also of striking out into exciting visions. It is a time of pain and yet a time of ecstasy, because so much is new and discovery of the new is always filled with both a wonder and a hurt.[15]

The configuration of the triad has a third element to make it complete in structuring a profile of a children's librarian. It relates to the need for a knowledge of the philosophy, organization and program of service that will make library service to children an entity and an integral part in the total structure of the public library. Embodied in the history of library service to children are the basic premises set forth by the early founders, from which evolved a philosophy as pertinent today as it was for its originators. It is imperative that children's librarians have a thorough knowledge of the historical foundations of public library service to children. This may be secured through a study of the contributions of such pioneers as Minerva Saunders, Caroline Hewins, Caroline Burnite, Anne Carroll Moore, Clara Whitehall Hunt, Alice Jordan, Frances Jenkins Olcott, Linda Eastman, Mary Wright Plummer, Effie L. Power, Mary E. Dousman, Alice Hazeltine and others. These were some of the women who established the principles and set the patterns upon which library service for children rests today. Their philosophical concepts for such service were visionary and creative. One sometimes wonders what their thoughts and their approaches would be in confronting children in today's environments. Perhaps Anne Carroll Moore would ask us to seek answers to the questions she posed in 1913 concerning the children's department in either a large or small library:

1. Does the work show elements of strong vitality to any one sincerely interested in children?
2. Is the book collection adequate to the cultural needs of the community?
3. Is the library service intelligent, active, and sympathetic?
4. Is the library *growing with* its community?

5. Does the library believe in its children's work as an integral part
   of a civic institution, or does it merely tolerate it?
In whatever exploration or pioneering we may do we must endeavor
to let our work be the center of as much as possible, and refuse to
let that pass for work whose affinity with life is narrow and whose
range of influence is small.[16]

Time does not permit an intensive view into the different aspects of
the preparation and performance of a children's librarian in organizing
and managing library service to children. Simply stated, there are several
components. Know the operational structure of children's services in
terms of communities served, the type of library system of which the
children's department is a component. Understand current organizational patterns for children's services in a wide spectrum of library systems and libraries serving urban, county and rural populations. Know
alternative organizational patterns that may be utilized. For example,
should the organizational structure of public services be based on type of
service offered rather than on the age levels of users? Or should there be
a consortium formed with related community agencies to provide a total
environment for children to meet their diverse needs and interests?

Knowledge of organization and management is enhanced with competencies in the art of research. Through research a children's librarian
evaluates traditional methods of service to determine those which are to
be retained and those which may be eliminated. Research will enable a
librarian to assess use and nonuse of services by children and adults concerned with children. Modules may be structured to identify publics
served and unserved and to determine needs and opportunities for extended services to the public. In the area of organization and management, a children's librarian has a responsibility to determine and to relate
new directions of service to reach the unreached.

Management of service to children requires a high degree of competency and skill in the sphere of collection building and maintenance. With
a wide variety of materials from which to select, a children's librarian
must consider the holdings in terms of their form, function and versatility. Carefully devised procedures for evaluation and selection must be
developed. In this respect the sentiments of an early pioneer of library
service to children, Clara Hunt, are as pertinent today as they were when
she spoke them: "If we are to follow instead of lead the taste of the children we must not flatter ourselves that we are anything more than clerks
whose duty it is to discover exactly what a customer wishes and then to
give her that commodity."[17] Once the children's librarian has made the
selection of materials, it is necessary to consider their organization and
control. This requires a knowledge of the cataloging and classification of

book and nonbook materials. Collection development also demands constant attention to maintenance and to the handling of current issues and concerns.

Pertinent to the management function is a thorough understanding of the theories and principles relating to the dissemination of information. With the glut of knowledge and information permeating even the environment of children, a librarian must be conversant with and understand the workings of networks, data bases and media programs. In this manner it will be possible to extend the availability of resources to those who use children's services. Insights into this realm and its importance for school media specialists have been cogently explored by Dr. Bernard Franckowiak in the fall 1977 issue of *School Media Quarterly*.[18] The applicability of information for children's librarians is unquestioned and this article should definitely be read.

Programs and services for children have been the high points of work with the youthful public. Numerous library studies, surveys and research projects have alluded to the great success of children's librarians in this aspect of their work. If the high level of achievement is to continue and ascend to even greater heights, then a children's librarian must work incessantly to improve competencies in programmatic tasks as new avenues open for exploration of new ideas and new approaches. Developing programs and managing them within and outside the library require an understanding of the administration of these activities within the total service of the library. Also, a children's librarian is expected to adhere to standards as they relate to the planning and execution of any program. Most important in meeting these standards is a need to conform to the fundamentals for excellent programming. These elements may encompass six essentials: (1) identify needs and opportunities, (2) define program objectives, (3) assess resources, (4) establish priorities, (5) determine methods of implementation, and (6) conduct evaluations. Success in conforming to these essentials will depend on an ability to develop and sharpen one's diagnostic, motivational and prescriptive skills.

A children's librarian gives service to the individual and to groups as well, both inside and outside the library. Diverse publics are brought into the matrix of service — schools and allied agenices, special audiences with special needs, adult audiences concerned with children or with materials for children, adult users and senior citizens who may derive benefits from services, materials and programs emanating from the children's department. The demands on a children's librarian are many and varied; yet enrichment and a recharging of one's potential are necessary if the creative spark is to continue. This is achieved in part through continuing education, affiliations with and participation in professional library, educational and allied associations. Equally enriching is the involvement in cultural pursuits and the intangible benefits derived from travel.

Thus, the triad has been completed. A configuration of a children's librarian has been postulated here from the vantage point of one library educator. Elements have been omitted which should perhaps have been included. Yet, through it all, if one were to ask: "What is a children's librarian?" a simple reponse could be: "How far does your vision reach in profiling such an individual?"

REFERENCES

1. Gardner, John W. Quoted *in* Ewald B. Nyquist, "Humanities and Arts in Elementary and Secondary Education; Towards a New Humanistic Emphasis in Our Schools," *The Bookmark* 29:288, May 1970.
2. Toffler, Alvin. *Future Shock.* New York, Random House, 1970.
3. Valens, E.G. *Cybernaut, a Space Poem.* New York, Viking Press, 1968, pp. 10-11.
4. Nyquist, op. cit., pp. 284-88.
5. Cousins, Norman. "The Arts Are No Less Basic," *Seattle Times,* Oct. 26, 1977, p. A12, cols. 3-4.
6. Silberman, Charles E. *Crisis in the Classroom; The Remaking of American Education.* New York, Random House, 1970, p. 8.
7. National Center for Education Statistics. "Enrollment in Educational Institutions, 1919-75." *In* Ann Golenpaul, ed. *Information Please Almanac; Atlas and Yearbook, 1977.* 31st ed. New York, Simon and Schuster, 1976, p. 739.
8. U.S. Bureau of the Census. "School Enrollment by Grade Level, Type of Control and Race, Fall 1974 and Fall 1975." *In* Golenpaul, op. cit., p. 738.
9. U.S. Office of Education. "Exceptional Children in Special Educational Programs, 1963 & 1973-74." *In* Golenpaul, op. cit., p. 737.
10. Allen, James E., Jr. "A Program of Priorities for the Coming Decade," *The New York Times,* Jan. 12, 1970, p. 61, cols. 1-2.
11. U.S. Bureau of the Census. "U.S. Population by Age, Sex and Race, 1975." *In* Golenpaul, op. cit., p. 703.
12. Lewis, Richard, ed. *Miracles: Poems by Children of the English-Speaking World.* Chicago, Bantam Books, 1977.
13. Baron, Virginia O., ed. *Here I Am: An Anthology of Poems Written by Young People in Some of America's Minority Groups.* New York, E.P. Dutton, 1977.
14. Farrell, Dianne, and Hayes, Ruth M., eds. *What Is a City: Young People Reply.* Boston, Boston Public Library, 1969.
15. Karl, Jean. *From Childhood to Childhood; Children's Books and Their Creators.* New York, John Day, 1970, p. 5.
16. Moore, Annie Carroll. "What the Community Is Asking of the Department of Children's Work in the Public Library," *Library Journal* 38:599, Nov. 1913.

17. Hunt, Clara W. "The Children's Library a Moral Force," *Library Journal* 31:c101, July-Dec. 1906.

18. Franckowiak, Bernard. "Networks, Data Bases, and Media Programs: An Overview," *School Media Quarterly* 6:15-20, Fall 1977.

ADDITIONAL REFERENCES

American Library Association. Public Library Association. "Goals and Guidelines for Children's Services," *Public Library Association Newsletter* 12:3-5, May 1973.

Benne, Mae. *The Central Children's Library in Metropolitan Public Libraries*. Seattle, Wash., School of Librarianship, University of Washington, 1977.

Casey, Genevieve M. "Alternate Futures for the Public Library," *The Library Scene* 3:11-15, June 1974.

Coleman, James S. "Schools Look to Society as a Resource," *The New York Times*, Jan. 12, 1970, p. 66, cols. 1-4.

Detroit Public Library. *The Changing Role in Children's Work in Public Libraries: Issues and Answers* (Post-Conference Report on a Pre-Conference Workshop, June 16, 1977). Detroit, Mich., Detroit Public Library, 1977.

Hechinger, Fred M. "The 1970's: Education for What?" *The New York Times*, Jan. 12, 1970, p. 49+, col. 1.

Kerr, Clark. "New Learning Looks Longer and Broader," *The New York Times*, Jan. 12, 1970, p. 49+, col. 1.

Nykiel, Joanne, ed. "Children's Services," *Illinois Libraries*, vol. 58, no. 10, Dec. 1976.

Profiles of Children (White House Conference on Children, 1970). Washington, D.C., USGPO, 1971.

Report to the President: White House Conference on Children, 1970. Washington, D.C., USGPO, 1971.

Sayers, Frances C. *Anne Carroll Moore: A Biography*. New York, Atheneum, 1972.

Warncke, Ruth. "Library Services to Children in the Mosaic of Administration," *ALA Bulletin* 61:1324-27, Dec. 1967.

CAROLYN W. FIELD

Coordinator
Office of Work with Children
Free Library of Philadelphia

The Children's Librarian as Viewed by Heads of Children's Services

"Only the rarest kind of best in anything can be good enough for the young."[1] These words are engraved on the Regina Medal, awarded annually by the Catholic Library Association for excellence in service to children by either a writer, publisher, illustrator or librarian. It is a goal toward which every children's librarian should strive.

What is a children's librarian in this age of the generalist, the information specialist and the computer? No one has defined it more concisely than Alice Hazeltine did in 1921: "A children's librarian is, first of all, a librarian whose vision of library work with children as an integral part of library work as a whole and as an educational movement is clear and compelling."[2] The children's librarian must have all the essential qualities of the librarian plus two important attributes: a liking for children as individuals and a keen appreciation of children's books. Knowing techniques for eliciting the patron's needs is helpful, but more importantly, the librarian must possess an innate intellectual curiosity to go beyond the superficial and to help the patron express those information needs. To do this, the librarian must be an avid reader of newspapers in order to be alert to current events and ideas. This is particularly true of the children's librarian, because children are exposed to the latest events and ideas through television and may want to know more on a particular subject but be unable to express this desire succinctly.

"Strong as a horse" is the motto of the children's librarian. Masses of children pressing against the librarian demanding the same material or information day after day requires a confident, relaxed and flexible mind, as well as a sense of humor that laughs with the children, not at them. Few children's librarians can sit at a desk and calmly dispense directions about where desired material may be found. One can, however, be physically and mentally strong and still lack the essential ingredient of a warm personality. Children have not yet developed a shield of inner defenses and the librarian must have a warmth of personality that welcomes and reassures each of his/her interest in them. The librarian must be fair in dealing with children and not play favorites.

All librarians should have logical, well-organized minds and public speaking ability, and this is absolutely essential in the children's librarian. Between 25 and 50 percent of one's working hours may be given to storytelling and talking to children and adults about the resources of the library. Public speaking requires poise and good judgment concerning one's approach, personal appearance and timing.

Where does this paragon gain the background required for a full performance on the job? With the explosion of knowledge and expansion of technology, both a college education and a graduate degree in library science are essential, as is continuing education. In addition to the regular courses in English, literature, history, science, psychology, sociology and public speaking, persons interested in children's work should have at least one course in child psychology and courses in as many languages as possible. The United States is still the melting pot of the world, but no longer are the immigrants eager to shed their language and culture to assimilate American ways. Today the librarian, social worker and teacher must often take the initial step in relating to and communicating with the immigrant.

It is during graduate study that the librarian should acquire the necessary training in reference and bibliography, interviewing techniques, use of technical equipment, principles of management, bases of work with community groups, and knowledge of children's books and folk literature. To become a storyteller, an individual must spend years selecting, learning and telling stories. However, the basics should be learned in library school. A course in storytelling is a valuable asset to every librarian in developing the ability to select, prepare and present a talk on any subject for any group.

The children's librarian needs an in-depth knowledge of materials (print and nonprint) and the ability to select and maintain collections that will provide information and advisory services for the community. Secondly, the children's librarian is expected to make an effort to help the child develop to his or her fullest potential. Service to the patron has top priority; it must take precedence over reports and meetings. The librarian who provides quality service to the individual will find this the best public relations policy for the library.

Creative programming within the library follows closely on the heels of service to the individual. In Philadelphia, the Vacation Reading Club is the only program required to be held in all children's libraries. During July and August, the librarian must meet regularly with small groups of children to discuss the books they have read and to entice them to broaden their reading interests. This arrangement gives the librarian an opportunity to get to know the child's individual preferences and abilities.

Storytelling programs for all ages, from nursery school through junior high, are encouraged. Weekly story hours may be too time-consuming, but any librarian can plan for a series of four to six story hours based on a particular theme or centered around a holiday. Once learned, stories can be used many times for assembly programs, at recreation centers, and with adults. The demand for preschool story hours has grown by leaps and bounds in the past thirty years. There is no problem getting an audience; the problem is finding time and limiting the registration. A common arrangement is a series of six weekly story hours of thirty to forty-five minutes each for children three to five years old.

Puppet shows, talks by authors or illustrators, special clubs, films and filmstrip programs are ways in which the librarian can also promote the services and materials of the library, as well as provide enjoyment and help to children in developing their imaginations. One of the most popular programs in Philadelphia is the Potpourri Hour, during which stories may be told, films or filmstrips shown, games played and/or a brief introduction to creative dramatics given.

Programming is not the only method of publicizing materials. Displays and exhibits are important. The librarian who is not artistic but has a good working relationship with other members of the staff may call upon someone with artistic talents for help, or encourage exhibits from members of the community. A display of arts and crafts by a Girl Scout or Boy Scout troop will not only provide a means of publicizing library materials, but will also serve as good community relations.

In a world where advertising is ubiquitous it is essential for the librarian to go out into the community. Schools are usually the first point of contact. Here the librarian can use common sense, enthusiasm, warmth of personality, and knowledge of library services, materials and educational needs in developing plans with the principal, librarian and teacher. Flexibility is essential in working with groups outside the library.

Next to the schools, high priority can be placed on work with the handicapped child, much of which must be done outside the library. Storytelling can be the first (and may be the only) communication with the child who is physically, mentally or emotionally handicapped. Often, the librarian's real job is to provide guidance in selecting materials and to suggest techniques for presenting materials to those who work with these children.

Working with the adults who work with children is the other aspect of the children's librarian's responsibilities. No individual can relate directly to every child, but every librarian should make contacts with the adults in the community who deal directly with children — parents, teachers, social workers, and friends. Talks to PTA groups, faculty meetings and community organizations must be planned along with programs for children. In order to work intelligently with these groups, the librarian must know about reading levels and methods and about the prevailing philosophy and methods of operation of the organizations concerned. Finally, the children's librarian must be an active participant in local, regional, state and national professional library organizations and, if possible, in related organizations such as National Council of Teachers of English, International Reading Association, booksellers' associations and others.

As experts in the field of service to children, children's librarians are committed to excellence and cannot operate in isolation. If the librarian can time guidance well, so that the child can be offered the proper material — whether it be folk or fairy tales, songs, science or adventure stories, or even handicrafts or games — to satisfy his or her curiosity just when that faculty is awakening, the children's librarian can maintain the child's curiosity and eagerness all through childhood. This is the best service that can be provided to a child.

REFERENCES

1. De La Mare, Walter. *Bells and Grass*. New York, Viking, 1942, p. 9.
2. Hazeltine, Alice. "What is a Children's Librarian?" *Public Libraries* 26:513, Nov. 1921.

WILLIAM CHAIT

Director

Dayton and Montgomery County Public Library

Dayton, Ohio

The Children's Librarian as Viewed by Library Administrators

What does an administrator expect of a children's librarian? Everything! Experienced administrators in public libraries look upon children's librarians as among the most professional of the various specialist librarians on their staffs. Children's librarians need the characteristics, understanding and skills which will enable them to relate both to adults and to children, as well as to other staff members.

The most essential quality of any librarian is that of intelligence. This characteristic is defined as the ability to adapt to a changing society and a changing institution. In addition to being intelligent, the children's librarian must be articulate, i.e., must possess an ability to express ideas readily. The children's librarian has to establish a rapport not only with children, but with the adults concerned with children.

The children's librarian, especially in large public libraries, must understand the current urban scene. The factors which operate to make each U.S. city racially, ethnically and economically unique are all important to the children's librarian, who not only will meet the middle-class and advantaged children but also must learn to work with the retarded, the handicapped and the poor. The children's librarian transferring to another branch in a large library system will often experience a complete change of juvenile public. This means that the children's librarian must be daring in his/her approach to problems and be willing to experiment with new methods and procedures rather than rely on the traditional picture-book hour, story hour or film program. This requires constant experimentation with creative ideas to determine what will appeal to children and what won't. Dramatic presentations, puppet shows, and arts and crafts programs have proven very successful in reaching children from preliterate homes. Books must be part of the program but need not be the beginning or all of the program.

Every large library staff composed of a variety of department specialists finds that at times they do not communicate effectively with each other. Children's librarians must convince the reference librarian, the cataloger, the bibliographer and others that they are not simply playing pattycake all day and that their job is as difficult and as demanding — physically as well as mentally — as many of the other jobs in the library. In relating to the administrator, children's librarians must be willing to apply businesslike procedures to their operation. They must help prepare and then adhere to budgets for staff and materials. They must, as must all librarians, learn to organize their work time and delegate responsibilities. An ability to supervise others, which children's librarians are not often considered to need, is actually essential in working with student assistants, members of social groups, parents and even children. In some libraries children's librarians have supervisory responsibilities.

Having considered the essential qualities of an ideal children's librarian, I will look now at some other desirable qualifications. Foremost is that of an orderly mind. People who are or often seem to be overworked are people who do not have an orderly mind. They flit from one task to another without finishing anything. They become increasingly disturbed over their lack of success and seem to be in a constant state of agitation. Children need the sense of stability derived from contact with adults who are in control of their own lives.

Appearance means a great deal to children. One's dress should be appealing and inviting to children; but that doesn't mean one has to be beautiful or handsome. Clothing should be chosen not only with the type of children contacted in mind, but also with the type of program being presented. A children's librarian may come as a witch for a Halloween program or in jeans to put on a marionette show.

Children's librarians should possess warmth and friendliness, but too many children's librarians are guilty of sentimentality. It is possible to have warmth without sentimentality. One needn't "love" children to work with them; one must care about them and enjoy being with them. Professionalism implies an ability to look objectively at one's work, fellow workers and the recipients of that work. This is sometimes difficult, but a good children's librarian can do it.

The ideal preparation for a good children's librarian is not easily definable. I have observed through experience with more than 100 children's librarians that the graduate degree is not the only preparation. Usually it is good preparation and enables many children's librarians to start doing a good job immediately, but in the long run it is not enough; one cannot expect to board a bus and ride forty years on a single fare. Continuing education is important for all librarians. Children's librarians prepared with either undergraduate degrees in library science or elementary education sometimes do as well as librarians with graduate degrees if they have in-service training and continuing education.

Developing adult interests is good preparation for a children's librarian. Music, art and literature (both adult and children's) should be included in the preparation of all children's librarians. Relating to adults in a personal, social and educational manner is part of being a complete children's librarian. A good children's librarian is a member of the adult community and shares professionally with other adults as an authority in work with children in print and other media.

One important factor in the continuing development of an ideal children's librarian is participation in professional activities and contributions to the profession. Simply working every day, whether it is in a library or factory, may be enough for some people, but it can become very monotonous. It prevents a person from looking at what can be accomplished through trying new things, relating to new people, accepting or inviting new ideas. Activity in professional organizations makes the difference between a job and a profession and is therefore very important in the preparation and development of a good children's librarian. Professional reading and familiarity with and knowledge of both adult and children's books is an enriching aspect of professionalism for all librarians.

The performance of a good children's librarian requires constant revision of methods of reaching children, parents, teachers and others. As society changes, children must be reached in different ways. A child brought up on "Sesame Street" cannot be reached the same way as children of twenty years ago. Neither can their parents, contending with problems of earning a living and providing for children in an inflationary economy, be reached in the same manner as parents of the more affluent 1950s and 1960s. A recent drop in library use led us to the conclusion that an increasing number of mothers are taking part-time or full-time jobs because of inflation, which cuts down on their own reading time as well as on opportunities for trips to the library with their children. Therefore, children's librarians must try new procedures and activities when the old ones fail.

All librarians, and especially children's librarians, should set goals and objectives against which they can measure their own performance. People often act out of habit rather than in an effort to reach a certain goal. We should ask ourselves what we are trying to achieve with our activities. A children's librarian should not put on a puppet show just because he or she is good with puppets, but because it enriches the lives of children and introduces them to a world of literature, art and music. Film programming is very simple in most libraries because films and projectors are available; it does not take much time and energy. There is nothing wrong with scheduling films, but the children's librarian must be sure that he or she knows why it is being done.

No matter how well we do our jobs, the task isn't finished until we let others know about it. Good children's librarians must relate their accomplishments and successes to fellow librarians, administrators, public officials and the people they work with in schools and recreational agencies. Their good work must be made known in order to gain public support. A good children's librarian must recognize and relate to the library system how the children's activities support and contribute to the library system as a whole.

Very often, competent children's librarians have become very good middle-management people. Branch library management positions have been filled by children's librarians who had been doing an outstanding job and thus came to the attention of their administrators and fellow staff members. Perhaps lost as children's librarians (although many branch librarians are also in charge of the children's section), they remain contributing members of the profession.

While attempting to delineate an ideal children's librarian, it is important to realize that not all children's librarians are cast in the same mold. One of the great joys of humanity is the diversity of people. The ideal children's librarian can have any variety of characteristics and a poor children's librarian can have the same characteristics but still be a poor children's librarian. Perhaps the characteristics which make the difference are hard to define, but it is this difference which must be cultivated.

NORMA L. ROGERS
Director of Children's Services
Urbana Free Library
Urbana, Illinois

The Children's Librarian as Viewed by Children

In an attempt to find out what children, i.e., patrons, think of librarians, three different techniques were utilized in the Urbana Free Library to elicit responses. The first was a brief survey, involving a one-line question asked of the children in thirty classes visiting the public library last spring. The second was a 2-page questionnaire filled out by some children who were regular library users, and the third was a 2-hour discussion with members of the Junior Critics organization of the library.

The first technique attempted to determine how children describe librarians. Children were asked to write a brief, even one-word description of a librarian. Most of the responses defined a personal quality, but a number of the children chose to list types of work performed by the librarian. The examples of work cited were almost entirely of a professional nature, with fewer than 10 percent describing any clerical jobs. Forty-four different descriptive terms were used, ranging from words like *happy, smart, intelligent, dramatic, interesting, understanding, cheerful, fun* and *polite,* to *mean, unfriendly, grouchy, weird* and *strict.* Some even thought of librarians as "pretty." The number of positive words far outweighed the negative, but of the variety of words used, 50 percent of the children described librarians as "nice" and another 20 percent as "helpful." The librarians on the staff should probably be quite pleased to find themselves viewed positively, but not much can be learned about the individuals or the profession from finding out that librarians are "nice."

Since the first technique proved to be generally inadequate, a 2-page questionnaire was designed which asked children about their use of the library, and their perceptions of the librarians, the children's department, and the adult department of the library. The children's interest seemed to dwindle quickly after filling in the data concerning themselves, and it is possible that the short, unimaginative answers reflect their dislike of filling in blanks and being tested. The written questionnaire was rather ineffective, other than revealing that the ideal children's librarian might also be "tough," and that given a chance to change the library, large fish tanks should be added.

The third step in this inquiry was to ask the children who were between the ages of ten and fourteen and were members of the library's Junior Critics book discussion group to meet to talk about librarians. As "junior critics," they had indeed discovered the true joy of criticism, and were very happy to criticize in any way that would be helpful. The children in this small group are regular library users and, given their frequent attendance and active participation, they are presumably children who are well served by the public library. These children were very much at ease expressing their opinions, and were reaching an age at which they were able to make useful judgments and incisive comments about the world around them. These children were knowledgeable and demanding.

The initial response of this group was that librarians should know books, like children and reading, like the work, and be helpful and patient. When asked what had been meant in the earlier survey by "nice," they responded that young children probably used "nice" to mean "helpful." In the words of one of them: "You can be nice and just sit there and hand out candy to the kids, but that's not helpful." What these children expect from their librarians is service.

One thing that stood out very strongly, both in the opinions of the group's members and in the earlier survey, was that many of the children regarded the children's department of the public library specifically as a place away from home and school, in the adult world, where they knew they would be welcomed. They were appreciative of librarians who came up to them and asked whether they could help them when they first used the library and were shy. A number of the children seemed particularly aware that librarians would take the time to help them. As one girl stated, "The card catalog is helpful, but sometimes you really need a librarian."

The Junior Critics group saw books and reading as a very important aspect of a librarian's job. They considered it important that librarians "always be on the lookout for new books," attend to the ordering of the new books, and read the books. None was so naïve as to think that librarians read all the books, but the group members believed it was very important that librarians read as many as possible in order to be able to know what is new and to recommend good books to children. They thought that this was especially important for librarians working with the younger children who might have a hard time finding good books. For themselves, these young people preferred to rely heavily on booklists, and wanted frequent annotated booklists of titles new to the collection. In the area of readers' advisory work, these children wanted librarians to be able to describe interesting books, but not to "give them a big explanation and almost give the book away."

The children had some difficulty dealing with what are called "good books." One boy described a book of which he said: "It looked terrific, sounded terrific, the librarian said it was terrific, and it was the dullest book I have ever read. It took me six weeks to read that book." When asked why he read it if it was so awful, he replied that it was a Newbery and he was reading it in order to get his name on a plaque on the wall. The group believed that it was the job of librarians to motivate kids to read, but concluded that librarians should have programs to interest children in reading which use good books, i.e., books that children are interested in reading. They agreed that librarians would be wrong in assuming that all youth want to read the same books, and should consider the children as individuals with distinct reading tastes.

Frequent reference was made to the need for librarians to be "well informed." If a child were to ask for a book about Fonzie and the librarian said "Who's Fonzie?" they would be very distressed with the service. Even the most avid readers are very television-oriented, and want books immediately on subjects they become interested in from television. Since television is an important source of their information, they insist that librarians be aware of it.

When asked about the educational background of librarians, the children had some very definite opinions. They thought that a librarian training program must exist somewhere, but that librarians didn't "have to go through a big school for ten years or something, like if you want to be a doctor or a lawyer." They agreed finally that librarians have to go through college, and had some recommendations about the kinds of courses librarians should take. They suggested areas of developmental reading, child development, anthropology, English, and social science, but "mostly about kids, because kids are the people that use the children's library." Their primary concern was that librarians be well informed and know about things that interest people.

In the area of job responsibilities, the children were basically unconcerned about the specific duties required to achieve good service. Collection maintenance was considered important, but specific duties were dismissed with "librarians have to get their paperwork done."

These children seemed to have a fairly clear picture of librarians, and could probably write a very acceptable statement of requirements and responsibilities for librarians. To summarize briefly, they thought that librarians should be people who care about children and like to work with them. Librarians should be knowledgeable about books and children, and should be well read and well informed in order to provide adequate reading guidance. They would have librarians obtain a liberal arts background, with a specific concentration of courses about children. They would expect efficient functioning, but also that the work be enjoyable.

Many assumptions are made about the library public; one of the most common of these is that "people think that librarians check out books." The children consulted in this case did not think so. They perceived librarians in very much the way we are attempting to project ourselves. These children indicated that they relied on librarians to help them to find books, to tell and read stories, to show films, to give puppet shows, to encourage them to read, and to plan programs and activities to interest them in reading. This study had progressed far past the initial stage before clarifying the fact that much has been accomplished when a majority of the children indicated personal satisfaction with library service by describing librarians as "nice." As one child said, "I think librarians are very nice and helping to all kids, and the library wouldn't be like a library without them."

It is important that children's opinions be expressed as part of an objective self-evaluation of librarians serving children, but it is even more important in the larger context of public library service, where the "public" does not always include children. Librarians must be aware of how often community surveys, reference use surveys, user satisfaction studies and image studies exclude children — or worse yet, do not include them simply because they were not even considered.

It is perhaps more difficult to obtain useful input from children, since they are unlikely to respond as easily to a written questionnaire as adults. There is a need to experiment further with asking children questions about library service, and then to share what is learned about worthwhile techniques. A fine study which would be useful to anyone working with children is the research report completed in 1977 for the Regina (Saskatchewan) Public Library.[1] The report should provide an excellent model for librarians attempting to obtain user input from children. A very detailed questionnaire was administered orally to children on an individual basis, and the data gathered provide much useful information on the ways in which children use (and do not use) the library.

Too often, input regarding children's use comes from parents and teachers working with children rather than from the children themselves. Questions must be redirected to the largest group of users, and this must be done soon if children are to be given a respectful hearing when the public library redefines its role as a community-based user-oriented organization in the next few years. There is a commitment to the child who wrote: "I think librarians are nice. They have a big responsibility."

REFERENCE

1. Fasick, Adele, and England, Claire. *Children Using Media: Reading and Viewing Preferences Among the Users and Non-Users of the Regina Public Library* (prepared by the Centre for Research in Librarianship, Faculty of Library Science, University of Toronto). Toronto, Centre for Research in Librarianship, University of Toronto, 1977.

FAITH H. HEKTOEN
Specialist in Services to Children and Young Adults
Connecticut State Library
Hartford, Connecticut

The Children's Librarian as Viewed by Adults Served by Children's Services

Who are the adults using, wanting and interested in public library services to children? What proportion of users do they represent today in library children's rooms? Do librarians perceive the effects of present-day stresses, priorities, understanding and indifference of adults on public library services, both in terms of access and support? Are librarians aware that the field of public policy relating to children has reemerged?[1] Answers to questions such as these need to be incorporated in an examination of children's services, present and potential, and of the "ideal" children's librarian.

The adults using children's services in Connecticut public libraries are not unlike adults elsewhere. They are parents, teachers (particularly from early childhood education centers), college students, professional workers from community agencies and service organizations, artists (including commercial artists, writers and film-makers), grandparents, and adults seeking beginning-level information or recollecting childhood joys. Some adults are sophisticated library users while others are unfamiliar with the library environment.

Current community profiles in Connecticut show a continuing trend away from centers of the suburbs and established neighborhoods. In the face of continuing economic and energy problems, planners for library services must look for ways to serve children in the growing outer rings of the suburban population. The exodus from the cities has slowed, but no significant reversals have yet been seen in Connecticut.

An analysis by the staff of the Central Children's Room of the New Britain (Connecticut) Public Library shows that roughly one-half of the questions asked in children's rooms are asked by adult users. Is this normal or unusual? Will it continue? What is the proportion in other libraries? Inquiries to other Connecticut libraries willing to respond will continue to be made, but what implications will the answers have for us?

At my request, Connecticut children's librarians have been sending lists of questions that adults ask in their libraries. This information should be regularly documented for continuing evaluation of services and for assessment of needed change or development. The questions show that adults clearly expect information about a gamut of materials, and want to find these materials available.

Adults want to find books which stress "situational materials" for young children, and for children in school, books which reflect individual interests and special needs. Adults request realia: toys, games, 3-dimensional objects such as puppets, costumes and musical instruments.[2] Requests for such material for young children are accompanied by questions about how to make them, and why and how to purchase them. Queries are made about games for older children, particularly for children who are visually handicapped, retarded or emotionally disturbed. Films, filmstrips and audio recordings are sought for a variety of reasons. Adults want information on child development, such as socialization (i.e., play needs and sibling relationships) and learning to read, as well as the means and materials in many media formats to facilitate these processes. Adults seek data about community and state resources for children's special needs and for generally available entertainment, education (especially nursery schools), and cultural opportunities. Adults ask about library programs for children, and for guidance regarding children's periodicals and literature.

Children's librarians seem to be viewed as media specialists, and as possessing information that satisfies various adult needs. The reference questions mentioned above are only indicators; performance measurements are lacking. Adult expectations obviously reflect existing services, which in turn mirror the impact of continuing education programs and the concern of children's librarians to serve pertinent information needs for and about the child. The state library's continuing education in children's services program emphasizes: (1) identification of children's needs and focus not only on services that meet those needs, but also on providing information to adults concerned with children; (2) community analysis; (3) development of community agency relationships; (4) use of community resources; (5) having an understanding of child development which enables proper use of appropriate materials and services; and (6) understanding the implications of the reading process.

Moving from the profile of Connecticut adult library users and their questions, I turned to informal conversations with adults. The question "What do you perceive as being the ideal children's librarian's qualities, qualifications, training and performance?" was asked of adult library users who were acquaintances with children of various ages, and colleagues from other professions concerned with children, including child development specialists, educators of teachers, reading consultants, child psychologists, social workers, mental health specialists, early childhood education consultants, pediatricians, and therapists. The libraries which these people use differ in size of community, kind and amount of materials, size and attractiveness of the physical plant, sophistication of services, professional competence and number of children's room staff, and in degree of support and understanding from the library administration.

The universality of the responses was a surprise. Two focal points emerged:

1. Expressions that the "ideal" children's librarian should know both the content and the impact of the library materials. In this regard, the "ideal" children's librarian should resemble the "ideal" teacher.
2. Strong feelings about the attitudes in libraries — that the "ideal" children's librarian needs to "like children"; "respect children and adults"; "be able to interact with different kinds of children, at different ages, and to see sharing and interaction with children as a continuing major priority"; "know personally the excitement of learning, recognize that learning is lifelong, that all children and adults have the capacity to learn"; "be able to see a situation from different points of view"; "use many materials and methods to get children to experience"; "be interested in helping children to think, i.e., to carry through with a thought"; "be able to provide the child with creative experiences"; "care about helping children who cannot read well"; "be nice to parents whose children cannot read and suggest ways to help them"; "make access to the collection always possible while the library is open — that is, no programming activity should limit access to the collection."

Interviewers noted that the "ideal" children's librarian needs to recognize that condescension is implicit as well as explicit — that adults are aware of facial gestures, body stance, lack of interest, inattention to needs, and tones of voice in libraries, as these apply to themselves, their children and others.

Other comments dealt with the performance and planning required for library services: extend out-of-library services since children usually require adult transportation to the library; develop wider staff resources, such as volunteers (both older children and adults), to augment existing services; develop graphics to cue parents about the acceptability of touching, playing with and enjoying library materials, as well as to indicate that it is normal for a child to want to take out a favorite title many times; determine the real needs and desires of the community and provide a variety of materials (not just books) to fulfill them; broaden the patron's awareness of local resources to encompass the many different agencies in the full range of children's services, and make an effort to develop multi-agency cooperation; find ways to effect interlibrary cooperation with materials and programming that involve children's competency in writing, film-making and book discussions, and include parental support program activities.

Adults do perceive the librarian's interest in their children and praise specific helping skills, yet the informal discussions elicited a dichotomy between the way librarians view themselves and the way adults concerned with children perceive librarians that has sobering aspects. These adult perceptions must be confronted. They also indicated that the "ideal" children's librarian needs to know how to write program objectives with regard for effective community public relations, do cost analysis, and put into regular practice interagency relations in program development.

In conclusion, some general implications should be clearly understood. First, it is vital for librarians to know both the content and the impact of library materials. This implies that the "ideal" children's librarian must realize that a child's development of cognitive structure has a direct effect on the child's learning ability, and librarians must know how that cognitive structure is developed. The librarian should know not only the theories of Piaget's stages of development but also the specific implications of these theories in terms of using appropriate materials and activities. Effective performance requires this. It would be a delusion to continue to ignore this training as a requirement for library school graduation. The fact that the child is developing is what makes services for children unique. It is necessary for the "ideal" children's librarian to understand the process of reading in order to be an effective supporter of children and parents. Continuing education is needed for further opportunities to develop content knowledge, and to learn ways of increasing public library effectiveness in designing program services and analyzing their impact. Secondly, the patron clearly needs sound humanistic development in the librarian.

These comments reflect not only on the children's services staff, but on the library staff as a whole. While training can develop skills in interpersonal relations and in the writing of job descriptions, personnel and performance evaluations, eradication of attitudes reflecting condescension and indifference toward patrons requires more than the mere presence of the "ideal" children's librarian.

The total of adult perceptions indicates roles, goals, services and materials. Children are dependent on adults for a long period of their lives, and they depend on adult perceptions. The children's librarian should strive to be an active, informed supporter of aiding children to become competent readers conversant with ideas and materials. Children should be helped toward an ability to express themselves in various media, enjoying stimulating interaction with adults as well as with their peers.

REFERENCES

1. Scott, Myrtle, and Grimmet, Sadie, eds. *Current Issues in Child Development.* Washington, D.C., National Association for Education of Young Children, 1977.

2. Hektoen, Faith, and Rhinehart, Jeanne. *Toys to Go: A Guide to the Use of Realia in Public Libraries.* Chicago, ALA, 1976.

ADDITIONAL REFERENCES

Andrews, J.D., ed. *One Child Indivisible.* Washington, D.C., National Association for Education of Young Children, 1974.

Bruner, Jerome, et al., eds. *Play.* New York, Basic Books, 1976.

Garvey, Catherine. *Play.* Cambridge, Mass., Harvard University Press, 1977.

Smith, Frank. *Comprehension and Learning.* New York, Holt, Rinehart & Winston, 1975.

Zigler, Edward F. "The Unmet Needs of America's Children," *Children Today* 5:39-43, May-June 1976.

MARY JANE ANDERSON
Executive Secretary
Association for Library Service to Children
American Library Association
Chicago, Illinois

The Children's Librarian as Viewed by Professional Associations

The title prescribed for this presentation seems to imply that professional associations are some sort of monolithic creatures that exist somewhere and are capable of having a "view." My experience, however, suggests that Pogo's observation on the nature of the enemy can be rephrased to describe associations: "We have met the association, and it is us."

Who is a children's librarian? Who are *we*? We have a multiplicity of job titles depending on where and at which level we work. In public libraries, we may serve as branch or regional children's specialists; heads of central children's rooms; coordinators or consultants for a system; branch, general services or bookmobile librarians; associate, assistant, or deputy directors. Some of us are directors of public library systems. In school systems we are the school librarians, library media specialists, instructional resource teachers, reading or language arts curriculum coordinators, and/or district supervisors of libraries, instructional resource centers or media centers. At the state level, we are consultants in children's services, librarians serving the blind and physically handicapped, institutional librarians and coordinators of institutional services. We may coordinate state library development services or school library/media services. Some of us are state librarians. Within state systems of higher education, some of us teach children's literature to child care givers, graduate library school students, potential teachers and teachers renewing their certificates, and to parents via television. We may be curators of special collections of children's literature in research institutions or deans of library schools. At the national level, some of us are editing library periodicals or reviewing media. Others are working in national or international research centers, and a few are writing and consulting. Some, like myself, are employed by children's librarians to work for them in our professional association.

One of the most significant achievements in the history of children's librarianship is the recent and continuing establishment of career ladders. It is true that some of the separatist mythology resulting from the early years of this specialization still lingers in the minds of a few administrators (and children's librarians) and continues to create problems. However, the barriers that for so many years denied children's librarians a promotion to branch librarian or district coordinator (without giving up their specialization and becoming an adult services librarian) have, for the most part, been broken down. Most of those drawn to or counseled into this field are women. Societal changes, including increased mobility, changing attitudes toward women and marriage, and an increase in the number of jobs, have made it easier for librarians to move from one geographical region to another. Because of this, horizontal patterns of advancement are now less difficult to pursue in the public library field. In the school library field, while the same changes might have had a similar effect, the tenure system and the often tenuous position of school librarians work against career ladders, except vertical ones.

Formerly, children's librarians were clustered in large cities; today they are found in every state — in small towns as well as cities. Whether there are many children's librarians in a library system or only a few, they are isolated from each other. They see each other only at meetings of the staff, committees or associations to which they belong.

Children's librarians are expected to possess many skills (evaluative, management, programming, etc.) that they often have had neither the education nor apprentice-type experience to develop. The attendance and responsiveness of children's librarians at the growing number of workshops, institutes and seminars on storytelling, puppetry and literature are evidence of their need to develop and refine skills, to share with and learn from one another.

Although each children's librarian brings his/her own unique personality, talents and intellectual capacities to the work, there are several characteristics common to nearly all children's librarians. First of all, they are caring people. They respect children and believe that children should have every opportunity to become literate, thoughtful, caring adults. Second, children's librarians are imaginative people; they have always been ahead, sometimes by decades, of their fellow professionals in finding ways to reach out to their clients. Third, they are well versed in the literature of their clientele, though unfortunately not as well versed in the nonprint media.

The professional organizations that offer children's librarians membership, from the local level to the national level, often are not meeting their needs, and in some cases are just beginning to develop the programs they would like to participate in and learn from. This is because such a pathetically small number of children's librarians belong and are actively involved in them. Often when they do belong, they carry their local type–of–library "turf" problems with them and structure their organizations in ways that perpetuate rather than eliminate communication barriers.

Unless children's librarians are located in a still-growing suburban area or a relatively small state in which the state library employs a children's consultant, they are unlikely to have any opportunity to preview, review and discuss children's materials with their colleagues. Some of these reviewing groups (e.g., in northwestern Washington state, the Bay area, southern California, or Missouri) have given or are beginning to offer service-oriented institutes and workshops.

Some state library associations have no children's services sections, some have a combined children's and school libraries section, others have combined children's and young adult sections, and a handful have a children's services section. While this pattern is beginning to change in a few states, the usual program offered for children's librarians during state library association annual conventions is a speech by a local or visiting author. While children's librarians are and should be interested in issues and subjects relevant to all librarians, the lack of specific content for children's librarians in state programs is an abysmal situation. That lack of content accounts to a large extent for low membership figures and lower attendance at state meetings by children's librarians. The major identifiable activity of many state children's sections is the management of a popular children's book award program. Two states have publishing programs that include materials for children's librarians.

At the regional level, there is a strong children's librarians' roundtable in New England, built by tradition and remaining viable because of good programs, short travel distances and heavy population concentration in the region. The Southeast, Southwest, and Pacific Northwest regional associations have very small children's sections and hold programs every two years — very much like the state association programs.

At the national level, the American Library Association (ALA) offers a complexity of structure unmatched by any affiliate association. Children's librarians from all types of libraries cluster in the Association for Library Service to Children (ALSC). Because ALA's structure provides for "type of library" as well as "type of service" divisions, children's librarians may also belong to the Public Library Association (PLA), the American Association of School Librarians (AASL) and the Association of State Library Agencies (ASLA). Most school librarians hold joint AASL/ALSC memberships or joint AASL/YASD (Young Adult Services Division) memberships. ALSC's members come from public libraries (41 percent), school libraries (28 percent), students and faculty of library schools (11 percent), publishing (2 percent), state library agencies (1 percent), retired librarians (8 percent), and miscellaneous foreign libraries, federal agencies and college libraries (9 percent).

Primarily because of staff limitations, prior to 1976 ALSC was able to offer members only one or two programs totaling about four hours in addition to the Newbery-Caldecott program during ALA's annual conference. In 1976 and 1977, the number of programs grew, and at least twenty-four hours of programs are scheduled specifically for ALSC members in 1978. ALSC also uses the preconference format every few years to present longer programs, sponsors the annual Arbuthnot lecture in various parts of the country, and is experimenting with regional workshops. The division publishes books, pamphlets, lists, and a quarterly journal (with YASD), and is preparing to publish a newsletter for its members.

Since all of these local, state, regional and national organizations are associations formed by and for librarians and others, why do so many librarians choose not to join, wait until they attain an administrative position before joining, join every two or three years, or join once and drop out permanently? Children's librarians first develop their perceptions of the value of association membership when they are in library school. If they meet faculty members who are active in library associations, who explain organizational goals and structure to students, and who give practical advice about participation, then it is likely that the students will become participants themselves upon taking their first professional position. If they meet faculty members who are anti-association, nonparticipants, and who refer constantly to associations as "they" or "it" rather than "we," then it is quite likely that the student will resist joining any association for as long as possible.

Economic conditions that affect jobs and disposable cash have a direct effect on membership figures in associations, as does any change in dues rates. These factors are offset, however, if a children's librarian perceives association membership and conference attendance as an indirect or direct way of developing contacts which may be of assistance in making job changes — vertically or horizontally.

One's employer (director, supervisor, or coordinator) can exert a great deal of influence, positive or negative, on who joins which associations. If the employer budgets for conference attendance as in-service educational experience, participates and encourages new as well as experienced employees to attend and participate, introduces them, and gives them support when they assume committee seats and offices, then the predisposition developed from positive library school experiences will be enhanced and the children's librarian will become an active member. The reverse is also true. Employers can and do discourage membership by translating anti-association attitudes into restrictive policies, such as requiring that a staff member be on two committees before expenses will be even partially paid, by sending the same administrative staff member(s) year after year, or by forcing use of vacation time for attendance. Coworkers can also have a positive or negative effect on attitudes.

Another factor affecting membership is whether the programs, activities and publications of the associations are perceived as professionally beneficial. The recurring question "What does it do for me?" is probably difficult to answer in most state and regional associations. In ALA/ALSC, it can be answered voluminously. It is difficult to answer, however, if the person asking expects a response only in terms of individual benefits because the programs, publications and most activities are also available (though at greater cost) to nonmembers.

Whether the association conveys an image of being "closed" or "open" to participation by new members has become an increasing factor in membership recruitment in the last decade. Associations which formally or informally convey an impression of being closed, cliqueish, fun only for the "in group," or "incestuous" in selection of officers, committee chairs and members should not have difficulty determining why they draw and retain so few new members.

The motivation which one would like to think is the major force in drawing members to associations actually ranks last in real effect. This is the idealistic motivation — the concern with the broad issues of librarianship and library service to children beyond the local service area. While one hopes that this motivation would be cultivated and nourished in library schools and in job experiences, it is understandable that immediate concerns (i.e., passing the course, getting the job, reaching the children in the community) are overriding and divert the vision. It is, however, a large factor in membership retention. After the first few years of membership, *if* the member gets involved with conventions, committees, or task force activities, the vision widens and commitment and caring begin to cross boundaries — beyond the library, the system, the county, the state and the nation.

While all of the above-mentioned factors affect children's librarians' decisions about whether or not and when to join a professional association, there are some factors beyond the control of association members. Although one may decry the fact that some directors of library systems, library school faculty and other potentially influential librarians are — and probably always will be — anti-association, there is little that can be done about it. Energy can be profitably expended toward ensuring that professional associations are worth the time and monetary support of children's librarians. The purposes for which the time and money is used must be examined critically. Recognizing their isolation and need for professional growth in skills and concepts, children's librarians must find ways to provide and support continuing education experiences at a variety of levels throughout the United States. Effective communications channels must be established during and between meetings in order to keep children's librarians in touch with each other. Bridges must be built between associations so that members see clearly the relationships among local, state, regional and national groups, and their opportunity to participate at all levels. Participation must be encouraged, perhaps even demanded, in committee work, task forces, discussion groups and on programs, via articles, letters and telephone calls. Concomitantly, the associations must be made flexible enough, i.e., less hierarchical, so that everyone *can* participate.

I have learned a good deal about associations since I first paid membership dues twenty years ago in my first month on my first job to the Dade County (Florida) Library Association; the county's Classroom Teachers Association; the National Education Association, and its (then) Department of Audio-Visual Instruction; the Florida Education Association, and its School Librarians Section; and the Florida Library Association, and its School and Children's Section. The past four years at ALA as a staff member have been, sometimes painfully, even more enlightening in that they have provided an opportunity to observe thousands of members giving, growing, learning, dreaming, discussing, deciding, trying, sometimes failing, and trying again. I am convinced as a children's librarian, as an association member and as your employee, that there is only *one* perquisite of association membership. It has no name except that which each of us gives it: it is the return for what we give to the association in active, concerned, enthusiastic participation. When we get it we begin to understand and to discuss what children's librarianship is about. The children we serve directly become no more and no less important to us than all the children in our region, our state, our nation and our world. It is through our associations that the clout can be amassed to do everything we can in their behalf.

Services

BARBARA S. MILLER
Coordinator, Children's Services
Louisville Free Public Library
Louisville, Kentucky

Our purpose in developing the services section of the Allerton Park Institute devoted to children's services of public libraries was to present an overview of what is currently being done in libraries for children, to raise questions about the philosophy motivating many accepted library practices, and to involve participants in a discussion of future directions in children's services.

It would be difficult to provide a comprehensive analysis of children's services in public libraries in terms of activities and programs because of the diversity of those activities and programs. As a means of resolving the difficulty, the subject is approached in terms of the library size, whether it be large, medium or small.

The writers of the following articles discuss library services to children as they are currently offered in large, highly organized systems; in medium-sized libraries, which may consist of two or more units; and in the small, frequently isolated library, which in itself is the sole purveyor of library services to a community. Within this framework, the authors identify special programs developed to serve preschool children, the handicapped child, ethnic groups and other services designed for special elements in each community.

BRIDGET L. LAMONT
Senior Consultant
Services to Children and Young Adults
Illinois State Library
Springfield, Illinois

Services of Small Public Libraries

The purpose of this paper is to discuss both state library agency services and children's services in small public libraries. I will present my perspective on some of the realities of these two institutions today and the effect of these realities on library services for children in those communities with small public libraries.

Small is a relative term and, no doubt, everyone has arrived at his/ her own concept of a small public library — from personal experience as a library patron, as a practicing librarian, and/or from the literature about the small public library. Elizabeth Gross's study defined small libraries as those serving populations under 35,000.[1] Informal conversations with fellow state library agency children's consultants lead me to define small libraries as those serving populations of less than 20,000 or even 10,000. Of the 597 public libraries in Illinois, 56.4 percent serve populations of less than 5000, as do 54 percent of New York's 737 public libraries.[2] Therefore, employing the term *small* in reference to libraries serving populations of less than 5000 is very realistic. I will refer primarily to these very small public libraries when discussing services because I believe they deserve some attention and should be remembered when planning for the future. Small libraries do not always indicate rural location — small libraries are also situated in maturing suburban communities.

In all sizes and types of libraries, resources and materials, physical space, staffing patterns and budgets, mold, if not dictate, service patterns. With reference to small public libraries, consider these aspects: (1) a library that is open only twenty or even twelve hours a week; (2) a librarian who is readers' advisor, reference and interlibrary loan librarian, cataloger, public relations specialist, and children's librarian (the oft-quoted phrases "other duties as assigned" and "total librarian" are certainly applicable here); (3) a library that has a yearly budget of $300 for juvenile materials; and (4) a library where the children's department is not a physically separate entity, but an alcove or section differentiated from the rest of the library by a sudden shift in the size of the tables and chairs or by the presence of mobiles and children's art work.

It is difficult to describe the attributes of the small public library in detail without creating stereotypes. Hearing about the very limited children's services and programs offered by many small public libraries would be disenchanting to some. While the librarians who keep these libraries operative (often from true community pride) are admirable, the children's services offered in many instances are depressing. However, discussion only of the small public libraries that offer exciting services and programs in spite of their size neglects the truly small public library that operates on a hand-to-mouth existence. It is alternately discouraging and fascinating to talk with library administrators who claim that if there is one aspect of library service alive and thriving, it is children's services. They should be taken on a tour of the small public libraries.

Librarians who work with children are often characterized by their creativity, but even creativity has its limits in the small public library. The persons working in these libraries are isolated — not simply from human contact or from other children's librarians (especially in comparison to the staffs at large urban public libraries), but from other librarians in general. In small libraries, there are several ways in which children's services are provided: (1) by a professionally trained children's librarian with paraprofessional or clerical support staff; (2) by a professionally trained librarian who is the library director and works in every service area as needed, but who delegates certain tasks to paraprofessional staff members on a daily basis; or most commonly (3) by a librarian who is not professionally trained and who works in all areas. Small libraries don't have the luxury of using one staff member for puppetry and another for the preschool story hour or the option of preparing mutual programs with a cadre of professionally trained children's librarians. At the "one-person" library, the librarian may be guilty of not dividing work time equally among all types of services, but as is only human, will tend to concentrate on a single area which seems most rewarding. An even worse situation would be having a librarian who is not comfortable with children. Even in the small public library with a professionally trained children's librarian, it is usually that one person who handles the selection of materials, plans and implements programs, initiates community outreach efforts, visits schools, and so on. However, there are compensations in that contact with the library director is frequent and the opportunity to be involved in the total library is easier, i.e., there are no layers of bureaucracy to penetrate.

Materials resources also are limited and ingenuity must be used to stretch the budget both for traditional materials and for those designed at the local level to meet a specific need. In the very small library, collections are print-oriented and it is not surprising to find older titles that have been donated and kept on the shelves to "beef up" the volume count or because the titles are still popular. (As methodologies are improved for accessing collections, small public library collections may prove useful as a backup resource to older titles by authors such as Cavanna and Du Jardin.) Ventures into nonprint resources occur most commonly in the areas of disk recordings, cassette, or book bags. It is not that the small public library does not want multiple copies, current nonfiction titles, etc., but budgets, space and staff to acquire and handle the materials are limited.

Programs in the very small public library are traditionally preschool story hours, films, puppets and summer reading clubs. As in so many instances, it is the librarian who makes the difference. They have learned, perhaps sooner than others, to use community resources for special programs and activities, e.g., depending on the local women's club for the preschool story hour series.

While there is much to say about the small public library, it is appropriate at this point to discuss the state library agency with respect to library services for children, particularly as they pertain to the small public libraries. It is those libraries that are most dependent on the state library agency. The role of the children's consultant has become synonymous with state library agency services for children and for children's librarians. Although a state library agency will always provide services to the small public library, it is safe to assume that agency services will prosper under the direction and coordination of a consultant whose specialty and experience is in the area of library services for children.

According to the *ASLA President's Newsletter*,[3] there are thirty-one state library agencies which list a children's consultant, but I know of only about fifteen consultants who spend at least 50 percent of their time on children's services. In 1956, Elizabeth Burr, Children's and Young People's Consultant at the Wisconsin Free Library Commission (and former public library consultant), wrote of "looking forward to the day when there is a children's and young people's consultant on every state library agency staff."[4] That day has not yet arrived, but rather than getting distracted by numbers, let us look toward improving, expanding and sharing our resources in planning for the future.

Traditionally, if many small libraries do not receive assistance from the state, they receive no assistance at all. Services offered by state library agencies to small public libraries include: booklists (which provide not only a list of resources, but an awareness of topics of concern to librarians working with children — a consciousness-raising technique of sorts); materials examination centers or rotating collections of new materials (an important tool for book selection, especially for librarians with limited budgets); continuing education opportunities in the form of workshops, regional meetings, etc.; statewide summer reading programs; lists, newsletters or manuals of program ideas; rotating collections or displays; core collections of juvenile books and backup resources of children's materials; and the undefinable area of consultant services — advice on collection weeding, remodeling or building a children's section, suggestions for new programs, and visits on-site to serve as a catalyst, reactor, troubleshooter or advisor.

An examination of the reports developed for the June 1977 meeting of the ASLA Consultants for Youth Services yields a partial listing of the following programs, all of which have value for the librarian in the small public library: a workshop on children with special needs; rotating exhibits of children's art; a lecture on the reviewer/critic's point of view by Zena Sutherland, third in a series of lectures sponsored by the juvenile book evaluation center; puppet kits for loan to public libraries; and a "Children's Caravan" that took to the road to present children's programs in seventy communities with the assistance of the state library agency's children's consultant. The last venture is interesting in that the local librarian had to participate in the puppet show segment of the program, thereby reinforcing the state library agency's role of providing continuing education and training for the local librarian. The children's consultant acts as initiator, coordinator, promoter, advisor, and lobbyist for children's services.

The efforts of a state library agency children's consultant, and the efforts of the librarian working with children in a small public library have been, will be, or should have been affected by library networking activities, particularly those with respect to the development of library systems. The configuration of service has been adjusted, and one result is the emergence of a "middleman" both as an organization (a system, regional library or area service organization) and as a human resource in the persona of a children's consultant. Where the state library agency children's consultant had an entire state to cover by direct contact, programs of service can be encouraged and improved by a library system consultant located in the region. Librarians can then plan programs and share ideas on a regional scale, which is also less threatening.

Training efforts will now be focused on a new group of children's consultants with the expectation that these consultants will work with the local libraries. The state library agency children's consultant will act not only as a resource person for the entire state, but as a mentor and consultant's consultant at the system level. There will be an initial loss of direct contact with all the local libraries, especially in the areas of basic service training and program demonstrations (which now will be facilitated through the regional coordinator). Where there is no regional children's consultant (and some regions will probably prefer to continue with the services from the state library agency without the expenditure of hiring their own consultants) the traditional pattern of service will be retained. However, the state library agency children's consultant can now, more than ever, focus his/her efforts on additional lobbying for children's services both within the state library agency and with other state agencies, as well as through coordination of the efforts of the system staffs. Too often, librarians working with children talk only among themselves and then wonder why no one takes them seriously. It is up to the state library agency children's consultant, and now to the systems consultants, to set the pace.

With the implementation of systems, it will be difficult at first for some to refocus their efforts, but we should not lose our focus completely. The goal of providing and improving library services to children must remain the same. F. William Summers once cautioned: "The children's consultant must have or develop some credibility and clout with the local library director and with key staff members within the local library. This is not likely to happen if the children's consultant is seen as doing exactly the same things and having exactly the same array of skills as the local children's librarian."[5] Similarly, the state agency's children's consultant is able to offer skills not expected at the system level and to compensate in other areas as needed. Subsequently, it is important for the local librarian responsible for children's services, the system or regional children's consultant, and the state agency children's consultant to define carefully and mutually the areas of responsibility.

Returning again to the subject of library services to children in small public libraries, I will make the following comments. First, it is essential to be concerned about the isolated librarians, particularly those in the rural areas. Many of these libraries will never be able to hire a professionally trained librarian, to say nothing of hiring a children's specialist. The very personal service to children provided in a small public library can offset some of the limitations in staff and resources. However, the child living in a small community has a right to expect total access to materials and exposure to excellent programs. The small public library need not be a limiting force because of its location. Ways must be devised to demonstrate to librarians and trustees what these libraries can and should provide in the area of children's services; in other words, expectations must be raised. This cannot be accomplished simply through workshops. Continuing education efforts such as workshops are futile when the librarian cannot attend the workshop because there is no one to substitute at the library or no one available to conduct the preschool story hour session that morning.

Secondly, the development of library systems in certain parts of the country will provide services closer to home for the small public library. Many programs traditionally offered at the state agency level can be planned and implemented locally, thereby involving more librarians. Programs attempted at the medium and large public library levels can be adapted with the help of the system and the state agency consultant.

The small public library should be a prime beneficiary of networking activities, including broader access to materials, so that a limited budget will no longer limit access to information and resources, both human and material. The small public library should also be a prime target for cooperative activities, particularly those between school and public libraries. This does not mean that efforts will be any easier, but on a smaller scale with a greater need they can be less inhibiting.

Spencer Shaw has noted that "contrary to some misguided conceptions, children need the most (not the least) qualified service to assure them the maximum use of a library and its resources to satisfy their limited, but ever expanding intellectual, social, and emotional needs."[6] To paraphrase, the most qualified consultants are needed at the state library agency level to meet the needs of librarians working with children, especially in small public libraries.

It is necessary to take into account both the positive and negative aspects of the very small public library and service to children in future planning. While we have been watching and discussing the plight of children's services in large urban libraries, things have been happening in those small public libraries which serve communities of 40,000-50,000 people in growing suburban areas, college towns, and the settled communities of middle America. Children's librarians — many of whom do not have the benefit of training in a large urban library — have seized the challenge of excellent library service to children. Their programs are not flashy, and the names of the librarians are not always well recognized outside their immediate areas, but they have responded.

There are two types of potential for library service to children in small public libraries: (1) the untapped potential in libraries which have not realized what can be done despite size, and (2) the potential of library service for children which has been demonstrated by the continually inventive programs of service for children in those small public libraries that have already met the challenge.

REFERENCES

1. Gross, Elizabeth H. *Children's Service in Public Libraries: Organization and Administration.* Chicago, ALA, 1963, p. 5.
2. *North Country Library News,* Oct. 1977, p. 1. (Available from North Country Library System, Watertown, N.Y. 13601.)
3. "State Library Consultants for Youth Services," *ASLA President's Newsletter* 7:44-48, May 1977.
4. Burr, Elizabeth. "The Work of a Consultant in a State Agency," *Top of the News* 12:21-24, May 1956.
5. Summers, F. William. "The State Program and the State Children's Consultant," *Top of the News* 29:313, June 1973.
6. Shaw, Spencer G. "Gambling with Your Future," *NCLA Odds and Book Ends,* Spring 1960, p. 91. *See also* _____. "Children's Services Operating Under 'Systems' Organization," *Library Trends* 12:44, July 1963.

AMY KELLMAN
Head, Children's Department
Carnegie Library of Pittsburgh

Services of Medium-Sized Public Libraries

According to Althea Warren in a 1939 report, a "medium-sized" public library is a library in a town with a population of 35,000 to 100,000.[1] A more contemporary statistical definition by Leon Carnovsky and Howard Winger, in an introduction to a 1962 conference on the medium-sized public library, termed it an agency "arbitrarily defined as one serving a local population of between 25,000 and 150,000."[2] The general idea in both cases remains the same. The medium-sized library is one that services a community larger than a small town or most single unincorporated suburban areas, and smaller than a metropolitan area.

The medium-sized library, usually housed in one building, is described by Winger as a "locally autonomous unit serving a single community."[3] However, the Harrison (New York) Public Library serves a population of almost 22,000 with a main building and a branch, and the Hayward (California) Public Library, serving a population of 98,000, also has a branch. Whether having one branch or two, the medium-sized library is a local unit loyal to its community and, provided that it is doing a good job, receives the community's support in return. These statistics translate into human terms. They define a community that is large enough to require and support a variety of services, but small enough to receive them in a personal way.

The staff in the medium-sized library is large enough to provide the expertise needed in special areas, such as technical services and work with children, but small enough so that the members know each other well and work together with a minimum of protocol and a maximum of effectiveness. The library staff and borrowers know each other by sight, if not by name. It is this personal relationship with the community that is a source of strength for the medium-sized library. The "children's services" serve both children and adults. Moreover, these adults have needs that may or may not be related to children.

Library services that have impact and visibility grow out of the community's needs. Some of these needs are readily articulated for the professional who is willing to listen. Others can be discerned by the observant librarian who becomes part of the community. The need expressed most directly by all ages is the desire for information — be it for a school assignment, a Cub Scout project, or a personal venture. The desire for recreation or entertainment is the next most visible need. The role library services play which is the most elusive and difficult to express is one of contributing to a better quality of life. Whether the community perceives the library as an agency that can enhance the quality of their lives, or even feels the need for it, is doubtful. Yet much of what librarians do, acknowledged or not, expands the mind and lifts the spirit.

Meeting these spoken and unspoken needs defines library services. The library materials certainly serve these needs. Traditional print materials are a rich source of information, recreation and inspiration. The librarian who knows his or her community and collection skillfully matches the two in the time-honored tradition of selecting the right book for the right patron at the right time. In addition, at the librarian's disposal is the richness of audiovisual media that reach people in ways that provide a different, but equally valid, experience. In order to exploit the strengths of audiovisual materials thoroughly, one needs the hardware to preview and use it. The medium-sized library should have the physical conditions necessary to show a film or listen to a cassette. Most libraries circulate the materials; whether the hardware can circulate is a budgetary item that librarians would do well to advocate.

In-house materials are a valuable and unique resource for the community. In an ideal medium-sized library (one having all the strengths outlined above), librarians are in a particularly good position to compile for borrowers a file of community agencies and organizations that work with children in any way. Whether patrons are looking for a counseling service or a crafts class, the library should be able to direct them. Indeed, a resource file can be of invaluable help to the library staff in combining program ideas and names of people with special talents who are willing to share them with children. Perhaps the community has a special landmark that needs to be interpreted for the children. A filmstrip or slide-tape presentation may be produced for in-house use and circulated to individuals and organizations.

As interpreters of the collection, librarians make it easy or difficult for patrons to use the resources librarians know are available. Whether called reference work or reader guidance, the librarian's obligation is to see that the child who wants a "good book" or information on a particular subject, and the adult from the television station who is looking for a story to dramatize, each get what they are looking for in the most effective form.

This point raises the question of access to adult materials by children. In a medium-sized library, where the staff members understand each other's goals, the problems should be minimal. However, unless the library uses a one-card system and/or has an official library policy, service to this age group is restricted. The desirability or artificiality of limited access to the adult collection, whether this is a good control or a cumbersome nuisance, are only two of the questions to be addressed.

Programming is another method by which librarians serve their community's needs. Children's librarians are incredibly good at it. Within the literature can be found a variety of imaginative programs to delight, inform and expand a child's world. For example, children tended a vegetable garden as part of the Vacation Reading Club of the Free Library of Philadelphia. The Wichita Public Library sponsored a Children's Dinner Theater featuring skits and improvisations based on stories and folk material.[4] In Manhasset, New York, the children's librarian trained teenagers with drug problems to help with the library's scheduled story times.[5] In planning programs, children's librarians should take advantage of the special place they have in the community to recruit the best human resources available both inside and outside the library to serve their borrowers of all ages.

Why do programs at all? Programs involve a lot of work. If they are to be successful, they must be well planned. I feel librarians do programs for the following three reasons:

1. Programs give the library visibility. They receive publicity in the newspaper, on television and the radio which puts the library in front of the community in a way that is hard to ignore. Programs bring people into the library; they are a means of reaching nonusers. Whether the nonuser returns or not, the library is no longer totally unfamiliar; it has been seen. Programs also allow regular patrons to view the library in a new light.
2. Programs stimulate the use of materials in the library. A puppet show can mean circulation of books on puppetry as well as of the story which was presented. A film on animals means circulation of books,

pamphlets and perhaps pictures of animals. To oversimplify, programs lead children to the materials. This goal is reinforced with displays and lists of related materials. The program serves as incentive to explore a topic further or delve into a new one.

3. The third reason is one which defies evaluation; if this is romantic, unscientific and unbusinesslike, so be it. Librarians do not know if the dancer brought in to move and talk to children in the intimate and comfortable setting of the library will touch the individual child or not. They do know that they are providing an experience the child might not have had otherwise. Expanding a child's world contributes positively to the quality of his or her life. It may be years before the impact of that program is felt. However, there is enough testimonial literature from successful adults about the effects of seeing an artist, hearing someone speak or reading a book as a young child to know that such programming is worth pursuing.

The case for programming has been stated succinctly by Margaret M. Kimmel: "If children's service goes beyond housing materials, if, indeed, it is to provide an opportunity for an individual child to go beyond what he thinks he wants to what he might want, stimulating, effective programs should be developed as a basic part of a library's service. And the program must be regularly evaluated and revised, because the program itself is a service, not an end."[6]

The medium-sized library exists in a community which is large enough to need a variety of services and to have a number of agencies which provide them, as well as small enough to allow the agencies to work well together. The library is in an advantageous position to cooperate with these agencies for everyone's benefit. Schools, medical facilities, social and recreational agencies, arts and special interest groups need the library's resources and the library in turn must ensure that its patrons know about their community's resources. One striking example of cooperative resource-sharing occurred in Woodbridge, New Jersey, where every Saturday afternoon the public library brings children's materials to the visiting area of the Rahway State Prison. This project is funded by a joint grant from the Department of Institutions and Agencies and the New Jersey State Library Development Bureau.[7] The possibilities for this kind of cooperation are endless and the prospects exciting.

Obviously, much of this is true of all libraries, regardless of size. Branch libraries in large cities can experience this same sense of community even without the freedom of the autonomous medium-sized public library. Everyone also has similar problems with evaluating present services and planning for the future. Librarians know circulation and know how to count heads and keep track of reference questions. If a program attracts a specific number of people, it can be deemed a success. What is more difficult to measure is the impact of library services. What is to be done about materials that circulate less than once every two years? Should they be swept off the shelf, or granted house space because when they are used, they are truly needed? Is too much staff time spent working with a social agency so that the library is not adequately covered? However the evaluation and planning are accomplished, the medium-sized library because of its size has a flexibility that is to be envied. If something does not work one way, it can be quickly changed. Word of that change can also be quickly circulated within the community.

There are other questions about the goals of library services. Are all librarians' efforts aimed at promoting the use of print material? Do they ultimately go back to the book? Are libraries moving in the direction of serving as a community center with a variety of activities? With all the options available to today's child, what role should the library play? Libraries are supported by tax money — how can they serve everyone? How can libraries reach everyone? Even if an instrument has not been perfected, methods of evaluation can be developed using techniques such as behavioral objectives and program-based budgeting. It is the library's goals, which once seemed so clear-cut, that still need examination and much thought.

REFERENCES

1. Warren, Althea. "Administration of the Public Library of Medium Size." *In* Carleton B. Joeckel, ed. *Current Issues in Library Administration* (University of Chicago Studies in Library Science). Chicago, University of Chicago Press, 1939, pp. 181-97.
2. Carnovsky, Leon, and Winger, Howard W. "Introduction." In _____, eds. *The Medium-sized Public Library: Its Status and Future* (University of Chicago Studies in Library Science). Chicago, University of Chicago Press, 1963, p. 1.
3. Winger, Howard W. "Characteristics of the Medium-sized Public Library." *In* Carnovsky and Winger, op. cit., p. 45.
4. "Program Potpourri," *School Library Journal* 23:26, Jan. 1977.
5. "How Books Affect Children's Growth," *American Libraries* 8:509, Oct. 1977.
6. Kimmel, Margaret M. "Library – Program = Storehouse?" *Top of the News* 32:52, Nov. 1975.
7. "Woodbridge P.L. Organizes Kids' Visiting Area Fun," *School Library Journal* 22:56, March 1976.

BARBARA ROLLOCK
Coordinator of Children's Services
New York Public Library

Services of Large Public Libraries

This paper is intended to trace the influences that affect children's services and to indicate what is and might be included in services to children in large metropolitan libraries. Children are defined here not as a separate species, a breed apart, but as young human beings with whom adults share their lives and whose prime differences from adults are their age, size and political inactivity.

In spite of concern about the status of children in today's society — the battered child, the unwanted child, the exceptional child, the institutionalized child, and so on — there is no "child power." The very best that can be said for children's librarians is that their actions are motivated primarily by their genuine liking for children and their dedication to sharing the child's sense of wonder at discovering the world through ideas recorded and expressed in various media. Through service to children librarians are afforded the chance to reach the child as an individual developing his or her own potential.

The management of large public libraries has been significantly affected by the continuing changes in the economic and social climate in urban areas. Administrators, in direct competition with other city agencies for the shrinking budget dollar, must strive to convince officials in municipal government that libraries deserve high priority among public community services. A recent report of library services in New York City is a case in point. The Budget Bureau of the City of New York critically evaluated the practices of three large municipal libraries in terms of management, costs, decline of circulation, underutilization of buildings, schedules or hours of public service, the number and use of paraprofessionals on the staff, general staffing patterns, library reporting methods, inventory and loss of material, and the use of computerization in circulation systems.[1]

It is little wonder that, in the effort to survive, a succession of internal changes is taking place in many urban libraries in the form of reexamination and restatement of library goals, and a general redesigning of the management structure. With more fiscal control being centered in local communities, the administrative shift has been toward decentralization, with most large libraries favoring organizational patterns which accommodate local needs.

Contrary to recent reports,[2] in many large libraries the current casualty of management restructuring has been children's services. The "1975 Directory of Coordinators of Children's Services and Young Adult Services in Public Library Systems Serving at Least 100,000 People,"[3] published by the American Library Association, revealed that in a 5-year period there was an increase of 109 library systems, and a concomitant decrease (40 percent) in the number of children's coordinators. An informal survey of nineteen of the largest libraries from California to the east coast showed that one-third of the libraries responding had downgraded the position of children's coordinator. Ten of the nineteen libraries had children's coordinators with advisory rather than line responsibilities. Children's programming or personnel training of children's specialists was transferred to another administrative office, which was generally newly created and higher on the management ladder. The move to regional systems often means that children's librarians are further removed from the supervisory role as head of children's services. Diminution of the authority or leadership role in children's services seriously threatens the growth of these services.

Two major developments which abruptly propelled large libraries into reorganization and self-examination within the last two decades have been: (1) the migration of population from rural areas to the cities, and (2) the unparalleled response to the social consciousness aroused by the civil rights movement of the 1960s. Attempts at accountability began when the relevancy of institutions such as libraries was challenged. The various interpretations of "relevance" resulted in a myriad of experiments, pilot projects and redefinition of the library's function in relation to its patrons.

These changes in library philosophy were also reflected in services to children. Although the idea of the serene children's librarian surrounded by a few attentive, cherubic faces was never the true one, the rapid growth of cities contributed to a frenetic pace of library services extending beyond the traditional walls of the library. Library programs for children took place in hospitals, playgrounds, museums, street fairs, community centers and even in department stores. The new emphasis on community outreach meant that children could enjoy storytelling over the telephone as in San Francisco or the Queens Borough Public Library, through "Dial-A-Story." Federal funding made it possible to launch such highly visible programs as the Queens Borough Public Library's "Operation Head-start," which focused on the youngest potential library reader, the pre-schooler. The Chicago Public Library was able to use a grant to transport 9000 children from 10 schools to its local branch libraries. This library also located information centers in storefronts where children could study in an informal environment.[4]

Schools were, and still are, important in the history of public library cooperation. The Philadelphia Project,[5] an experiment involving the staff of the Free Library of Philadelphia, educators in the school community and students of target schools, helped to call attention to the effects of library use at various stages in the development of school children.

Today, however, the schools have become as fiscally vulnerable as the large public libraries. The early growth of media centers in the schools was dramatic. In New York State, media centers were mandated for every elementary school — but the position of the media specialist was not! The problem with this state of affairs was never more evident than during the period of New York City's imminent bankruptcy.

In 1975 the New York Public Library applied for and received an ESEA Title II Special Purpose grant of $60,000 for use in its George Bruce branch.[6] The branch and three schools in District 5 (Manhattan) were to be part of a project demonstrating an exemplary program of school and public library cooperation in which children would have access to information and materials both related to their school curriculum and for enriching it in their free time after school hours. Actually PS 125, the only public school in the project, already had one of the best-equipped media centers in the area, housing a large selection of nonprint media and equipment. The strength of the library branch in the area was its good book collection. The grant money enabled the library to enlarge its meager nonprint collection and to add materials geared to the curriculum needs of the students.

Also in 1975 budget cuts were made which affected all public agencies in New York City. The three schools involved in the project lost vital personnel. Both the public school's media specialist and the branch library's children's librarian were removed from their jobs and the school media center was closed. The public library administration felt a commitment to the project, however, and despite curtailed service hours, provided sufficient staff support to enable a continuing dialogue between the children's librarians and school teachers, and ensured access to library materials for the children in the schools. Today, with the help of CETA and other government funding, the children's librarian position has been reinstated, the media specialist has returned to open the school's media center, and the resource-sharing project progresses with some continuity.

In urban areas the children's librarian works closely with a variety of agencies. Brooklyn Public Library's recent publication, "Get Ready to Read," illustrates one area of cooperation large libraries are increasingly interested in exploring: the business community. The printing of this simple but helpful brochure was financed by a local bank, thus making it possible for the library to distribute thousands to parents of preschool children. The schools played a part, too, by supplying original art work of students from one of the Brooklyn school districts.

National awareness of the needs of children with mental, emotional or physical handicaps has influenced library services in the urban centers. The Free Library of Philadelphia, for example, is engaged in a LSCA project for service to the deaf, and Philadelphia branch libraries now have children's books about deafness and stories in signed English.[7]

What really distinguishes the children's department in large public libraries from its counterpart in smaller systems is the diversity of its users. The population shift to the cities mentioned earlier meant a new constituency for the urban library, many of which were poor, economically and educationally disadvantaged and from minority groups: blacks, Hispanics and poor rural whites. Most of the adults in these groups viewed traditional institutions with suspicion since they found little representation or reflection of their own cultural patterns in them. One-third of the library users from these groups were identified as school children, and two-thirds were nineteen years of age or younger. Children's specialists discovered that adults in these groups are best approached through their children.

Bibliographies of bilingual materials have grown out of work with the large Spanish-speaking population in the south Bronx of New York City, as have bibliographies on the black experience from work with children in Harlem and Chicago, who had a dearth of material about their own people. Libraries in the west and southwest have developed similar materials for their large Chicano population, and encouraged use of materials that promote intercultural understanding among the various groups living in their communities.

The information explosion has, however, added another responsibility to the children's specialist. The various forms in which information now comes — films, filmstrips, cassettes, audiovisual kits, and toys — add another dimension to the duties of the children's specialist, who must now develop areas of expertise in judging framed prints, posters, and so on for selection and use with children. The view of the library's administration regarding the importance of these materials helps to determine the budgeting for their acquisition.

Mention should be made of another of the effects of the large libraries' thrust to reach the "unserved." As more projects developed and increasing emphasis was placed on "new directions," it became apparent that the supply of professional staff was not infinite. In fact, long before the erosion of leadership in the services was noticeable, there was a shortage of children's librarians in the urban libraries. This meant that in these libraries, which often served as training centers for the profession, there was a steady exodus of personnel within given periods, and the continuity and stability of service rested at the leadership level. In-service training programs became an important factor in the total program of services to children. The complexities brought about by the new social consciousness of the 1960s and the later diminishing budget resulted in a more comprehensive definition of the responsibilities of the children's librarian and the emergence of the paraprofessional.

In some cities, it was discovered that a paraprofessional worked well when he or she was a member of the community or ethnic group being served. They helped to ease the institutional barrier while interpreting the library to the community. While some worked especially well with children, they lacked the specialized training and background to assume the full responsibilities of the trained librarian. But in times of fiscal crisis, paraprofessionals have been left in charge of small units and have assumed responsibilities long before adequate training and definitions of duties are given. This further diminishes service not only to children but to adults, teachers, students of children's literature, and parents.

The new direction indicated, then, is simply this: How sacrosanct is storytelling, for example, as part of the librarian's duties? Is it really *de rigueur* that a librarian tell stories when her forte may be informing the local PTA about the trends in children's literature? In one library, long before labor union contracts carefully delineated those activities which the professional or nonprofessional may perform within their respective job classifications, at least two of its notable storytellers were in the clerical or paraprofessional category. Continuing examination of the nature of the professional librarian, the generalist and the paraprofessional now consumes the "trainer's" time in large public libraries. Implications may be drawn for the old-line children's specialists who are sometimes unreceptive to the support roles of this new and emerging personnel phenomenon in library services to children, the paraprofessional.

IMPLICATIONS FOR THE FUTURE

In many large libraries, service to children has kept pace with the expanding services being offered to adults, and the unique demands of the diversified groups in the cities have confirmed the need for trained professionals with background in the literature and program needs of children and their parents. Weakening of children's services weakens the totality of the library program.

Large libraries may well have to develop a mechanism for securing funding for surveys of library functions if libraries are continually to compete with other municipal services. Cost analysis for children's services would form an important component in such studies and, vital to such an analysis would be a comprehensive user survey involving both children and their parents.

Networking and resource-sharing are important trends in the delivery of library services. Children are too often limited to the media resources of one agency or one department within an agency. In spite of the generally limited mobility of children, they should be allowed the option of access to materials which several cooperative projects have demonstrated as possible. Children do have vast information needs.

Children's librarians should become involved in literacy programs, become more knowledgeable about how children learn to read, and explore ways in which public library resources can be used or shared in the school community to combat the growing problem of illiteracy. Children's specialists and other library specialists might form a partnership with other educators to fight illiteracy. Parent education should also become an important component of work with children in approaching literacy problems. Parents are often unaware of their primary role in the educational process.

The potential for community support of services to children is seen by the growth of "friends" groups. The business community and other community sources should be encouraged as advocates for library services. Some administrators have pointed out that the cost-inefficient story hour program should be weighed against programs supported and supplied by volunteers. These volunteers are generally professionals such as performers, authors, artists or local residents with special skills.

Children's specialists need to develop political sophistication and to take the initiative in maintaining communication with administrators. Budget-making decisions which affect children's services are not beneficial to the service or the library without the involvement of the children's library specialist.

Attendance at conferences and institutes such as this suggests the rightful preoccupation of children's specialists with the need for communication and continuing education. Children's specialists/consultants of metropolitan libraries around the country have for years felt the need to meet informally to exchange ideas, even though their systems and administrative styles differ. It is indeed true that services to children in large libraries reflect all the current forces of change which affect library services to children everywhere.

REFERENCES

1. *See* "Comments on the Budget Bureau Report Titled 'A Study of the Branches of the New York City Library System' (prepared by the Office of the Branch Libraries of the New York Public Library)." New York, The New York Public Library, Nov. 1974. (Unpublished report.)

2. Farrell, Dianne. "Children's Services — Unexplored Issues and No Answers," *PLA Newsletter* 16:3+, Fall 1977.

3. Children's Services Division. "1975 Directory of Coordinators of Children's Services and Young Adult Services in Public Library Systems Serving at Least 100,000 People." Chicago, ALA and Division of Library Programs, U.S. DHEW, Bureau of Libraries and Educational Technology, 1970.

4. Eastlick, John T., and Schmidt, Theodore A. "The Impact of Serving the Unserved on Public Library Budgets," *Library Trends* 23:603-14, April 1975.

5. Benford, John Q. "The Philadelphia Project," *Library Journal* 96:2041-47, June 1971.

6. Baker, D. Philip. *School and Public Library Media Programs for Children and Young Adults.* Syracuse, N.Y., Gaylord Professional Publications, 1977, pp. 237-41.

7. Field, Carolyn W. "Program — Activities — Selected Highlights, September-December 1976." Philadelphia, Office of Work with Children, Free Library of Philadelphia, Jan. 14, 1977. (Unpublished report.)

AMY KELLMAN
Head, Children's Department
Carnegie Library of Pittsburgh

Services to Preschoolers and Adults

"Children in the library/ stand no longer by your knee./ Children turning page on page/ are not children, have no age./ Have no heed, no hand to take;/ go at will, with whom they like."[1] These lines from Norma Farber's poem describe the self-confident and independent modern child, who approaches the library as one more experience in a busy life. For the preschooler, who by virtue of age shares the library experience with an adult, some wide-eyed wonder may still remain.

For librarians the word "preschooler" has taken on a new definition. It no longer refers to the three- to six-year-old child. From birth on the child has a place in the library's scheme of things. For instance, Toronto, Ontario hospitals send the new mother home with a pamphlet from the Mississauga Library System describing sources in the library that will help her cope with and enjoy her baby.[2]

In short, the public library is involved in "early childhood education," aptly defined as being "concerned with the total development of each young child from birth — with all his components for growth, including physical, intellectual, emotional, social and adaptive."[3] Materials are chosen with child's developmental and recreational needs in mind, creating an increased interest in realia, especially toys that can provide the concrete experiences to which the very young child responds best. Toy-lending arrangements of all kinds have been tried.

The Clovis (New Mexico) Public Library has developed The Parent/ Child Toy Lending Library that operates on the theory that "the parent is the most significant teacher for the child, and the preschool child who from an early age (almost from birth) is deliberately involved in the process of discovering and learning will be able to deal more effectively with the formalized learning procedures of schooling."[4] In addition to providing toys, the library runs a 5-week series of classes for parents to introduce the basic toys and explain the learning skills which they develop.[5] In Pittsburgh, the public library has recently established ties with a toy lending library run by volunteers. Instead of starting from scratch, the library moved into an established program and the volunteers received badly needed staff support and special programming.

In addition to the traditional preschool story hours, librarians are experimenting with a variety of programs ranging in scope from the Erie (Pennsylvania) Media Library for Preschoolers with its emphasis on a flexible environment and continuous, spontaneous programming[6] to the libraries with occasional one-time activities. The May 1977 *School Library Journal* describes two activities geared to the very young child. The Greenburgh (New York) Public Library runs a "Storytime for Toddlers."[7] Language development, verbal stimulation and socialization skills for two-year-olds come out of this activity, in addition to enjoyment for both the children and their parents. Craft classes for two- and three-year-olds were tried by children's librarians in Fairfax County, Virginia.[8] The experience itself, regardless of whether it ends in a finished product, is another opportunity for parents, children and the librarian to interact.

These programs are examples of ways to provide young children with verbal and visual stimulation. The cliché that play is the child's work is true, and the library has the potential to make this work more satisfying and productive. Library service to the very young is limited only by the librarian's imagination. Developing a program for this age group within the physical and financial confines of individual libraries is a challenge.

In our library, we have approached it from different directions in a piecemeal fashion. For example, the traditional preschool story time has not changed much in format, although we have experimented with moving the time from morning to early evening. Would some combination of realia and the verbal create a valuable experience? Since language development is so crucial in the early years, it is wise to rethink the format of one of the library's most prized programs — the preschool story hour.

There is a long way to go with service to the preschooler. Programs are normally dependent on parent participation. The preschooler is a physically, mentally and emotionally demanding individual; thus, parents need all the support they can get. Simultaneous programming for parents is one way to support both groups without causing a babysitting problem. This requires more staff, of course, which is a problem in some libraries. It is not impossible, however; for instance, a capable guest speaker can be introduced and left to speak while the librarian works elsewhere with the children. Careful planning, as usual, is the rule.

That children's librarians are providing parent support programs is obvious not only from the literature, but also from conference activity. Those who attended the 1977 ALA conference in Detroit were exposed to a Parent Support Program Sampler. Librarians were able to examine it at their own pace and to question the people involved in its various components.

Through the Association for Library Service to Children (ALSC), ALA has provided numerous ideas for programs with preschoolers and parents. *Start Early for an Early Start: You and the Young Child* and *Opening Doors for Preschool Children and Their Parents*[9] are resource guides published by ALSC's Preschool Services and Parent Education Committee. *Toys to Go: Use of Realia in Public Libraries,*[10] edited by Faith Hektoen and Jeanne Rinehart, is another useful tool. There are resources, especially in the print area, available to children's librarians, but as Sandra Sivulich, writing in *PLA Newsletter,* states: "Wouldn't it be great if there was a 'Standard Catalog' objectively annotating what is needed for a basic pre-school library (other and in addition to books, that is)?"[11]

What kind of support programming should the children's librarian develop? Should all the programs, whether individual or in a series format, relate to library materials? Is the whole world of the preschooler grist for the mill, or can other agencies better handle questions about medical problems, for example? Do libraries need more cooperative programming? Should libraries have cooperative programming among departments in a library? How much of a referral function can children's services handle? In Parma, Ohio, an information and referral service for parents of preschool children has been carefully developed.[12] Should libraries providing this service follow up requests for information to ensure that parents get the help they need? This kind of information and referral service, with its attendant problems of updating and followup, is, of course, neither unique to children's services nor restricted to requests for preschool children's needs.

Other adults — educators, social workers, health personnel, and students — also benefit from parent support services and use materials for and about children. A parent-teacher collection housed in the children's department is an increasingly familiar sight. This raises the question of whether books about child development, as well as books about materials for children, should be housed in the children's room. If this is physically impossible or philosophically undesirable, what is the best way to ensure access to this body of information? Are children's librarians sufficiently knowledgeable about these materials to do effective reference work with the adult community? Librarians are familiar with the adult refugee from the science and technology department who knows there must be a simple and clear explanation of how car engines work, or with the journalist needing basic information about an unfamiliar topic. Materials for children are the answer for these people. How do librarians let the adult community know? Smaller libraries have experimented with interfiling adult and juvenile nonfiction. When this is not possible, how do children's librarians promote access?

During a discussion at the 1977 Preconference on Children's Services in Public Libraries in Detroit, it was suggested that children's librarians were searching for a clientele when they served preschoolers and adults. That is not a question I wish to raise at this institute. I believe in service to preschoolers and adults. Moreover, librarians have always served these groups; now they are doing it better. The increased sophistication and range of services available to preschoolers and adults, especially parents, are highly visible both in the literature and in the local community. Individual creative efforts to serve this clientele, whose needs seem so divergent yet who are found together in so many settings, are happening around the country. It still remains, however, for the profession to articulate a policy that will generate a statement of needs and a statement of process.

REFERENCES

1. Farber, Norma. "Children in the Library," *The Horn Book Magazine* 52:269, June 1976.
2. "Welcoming New Arrivals," *American Libraries* 8:481, Oct. 1977.
3. Hektoen, Faith H., and Rinehart, Jeanne R., eds. *Toys to Go: A Guide to the Use of Realia in Public Libraries.* Chicago, ALA, 1976.
4. Baker, D. Philip. "Exemplary Media Programs," *School Library Journal* 23:23-27, May 1977.
5. Ibid., p. 25.
6. Sivulich, Kenneth G., and Sivulich, Sandra S. "Media Library for Preschoolers; a Service of the Erie Metropolitan Library," *Top of the News* 31:49-54, Nov. 1974.
7. Markowsky, Juliet K. "Storytime for Toddlers," *School Library Journal* 23:28-31, May 1977.

8. Lane, Marie I. "Practically Speaking: Preschool Craft Activities," *School Library Journal* 23:43, May 1977.

9. Johnson, Ferne, ed. *Start Early for an Early Start: You and the Young Child.* Chicago, ALA, 1976; and Preschool Services and Parent Education Committee, Children's Services Division. *Opening Doors for Preschool Children and Their Parents.* Chicago, ALA, 1976.

10. Hektoen and Rinehart, op. cit.

11. Sivulich, Sandra. "Idea Exchange: Public Libraries and Early Childhood Education," *PLA Newsletter* 16:4-5, Spring 1977.

12. Blaha, Linda. "An Information and Referral Service for Parents of Preschool Children," *Top of the News* 33:360-62, Summer 1977.

BARBARA ROLLOCK
Coordinator of Children's Services
The New York Public Library

Services to Ethnic and Racial Minority Groups

It was remembrance of childhood experiences in the library that prompted author Bel Kaufman to write in defense of libraries: "It seems to me that especially now, when there are so many people in our city [New York] whose language is not English, whose houses are barren of books, who are daily seduced by clamorous offers of instant diversion, especially now we must hold on to something that will endure when the movie is over, the television set broken, the class dismissed for the last time."[1]

The immigrant group from which Kaufman came found that schools and libraries were the key which opened the door for achieving the "American dream." Libraries played an important part in the educational and cultural lives of the early immigrants for whom life was difficult, but for whom the formula for success lay in assimilation into the American mainstream — a goal that was attainable. For later or other groups, however, some whose roots lay deep in the American soil, the very nightmare of coexistence foretold that the dream, in the words of the poet, was not only "deferred," but would be denied.[2]

The effects of the civil rights movement in arousing the social awareness of various institutions whose prime responsibility was services to people have already been mentioned. Not the least of these institutions are libraries. When libraries embraced "outreach" to the "unserved" (a euphemism for those groups later identified as the principal minority racial and ethnic groups in the country), they were approaching people who shared common bonds: poverty, undereducation, lack of skills, and disenchantment with promises that would not be fulfilled.

It is to the credit of the profession that libraries undertook this tremendous task. The time was right, politically and financially. Government funding, foundation grants and other private monies were available to many institutions — to prove what? That dollars could compensate for educational gaps? That dollars could purchase standard English speech and provide an entry into the mainstream of American life? That dollars could provide or at least contribute to the evolution of a hyphenated-American, whose reception in society would indeed be eased by the time and efforts now being focused on his/her differing culture? Or, more importantly, that dollars would really erase century-old attitudes toward those highly visible individuals whose traditionally lower economic and social status had previously rendered them invisible?

As we read the professional literature with present hindsight, the recurring thought during these times of financial pressures is: How valid were the means used? How cost-effective the monies spent? What was the ratio of return in the achievement of this noble library goal to "serve the unserved"? Researchers have here a meaty subject in assessing the true effectiveness of these programs.

Before embarking in other directions, we must assess our accomplishments: today, the preschooler, the senior citizen; tomorrow, the exceptional — next year, all red-haired, brown-eyed people? What have we learned? How many from the homes Bel Kaufman mentions actually reaped the benefits of outreach? How many Bel Kaufmans did we locate whose use of libraries eased the language barriers? How many of us attempted attitudinal studies to measure the effectiveness of the library's carefully prepared bibliographies mentioned earlier?

Actually, before black became beautiful, pioneers in the library profession, Charlamae Rollins in Chicago and Augusta Baker in New York,[3] had established guidelines for work with children and adults and had attempted to arouse a sense of intercultural understanding and sensitivity through identification of certain elements in children's books. The criteria they cited focused on the dangers of stereotyping and the absence of positive images for black children in the literature of the day, and their criteria for evaluation were later applied and researched in more formal studies.[4] There is no doubt that later studies and books on the subject of racism[5] and stereotyping have had a tremendous impact on the publication of children's books from 1965 to the present.

Studies about the effect of cultural differences in language development, such as that by Doris R. Entwisle,[6] would perhaps further illustrate whether our approaches to children of minority groups and non-English-speaking backgrounds are valid. While we use and introduce literature today so that the child will have a good positive self-image, do we really know how children see themselves? Some studies indicate that children initially come to us with firm positive images.[7] Children as individuals do need reassurance about their place in the family, but they also need to learn about others. It is not inconceivable for inner-city children to understand Anne Frank, or for children from low-income families to appreciate Harriet in Fitzhugh's story *Harriet the Spy*. Each of these stories brings the common human experience within the realm of all children regardless of their socioeconomic origins.

Perhaps it is sufficient that at least one child reader was able to reach adulthood and publicly to declare the influence of libraries on her life. As Bel Kaufman describes it, the librarian was not concentrating on her special needs or background. She was available, knowledgeable about books and efficient in her ability to disseminate information. Nevertheless, she had touched a child who had merely come to read.

REFERENCES

1. Kaufman, Bel. "The Liberry," *The New York Times,* July 23, 1976, p. A21.

2. Lipsman, Claire K. *The Disadvantaged and Library Effectiveness.* Chicago, ALA, 1972.

3. Rollins, Charlamae H. *We Build Together; A Readers' Guide to Negro Life and Literature for Elementary and High School Use.* Urbana, Ill., National Council of Teachers of English, 1967, pp. ix-xxvii; and Baker, Augusta. "Guidelines for Black Books: An Open Letter to Juvenile Editors," *Publishers Weekly* 196:131-33, July 14, 1969.

4. Agree, Rose H. "The Black American in Children's Books: A Critical Analysis of the Portrayal of the Afro-American as Delineated in the Contents of a Select Group of Children's Trade Books Published in America from 1950-1970." Ph.D. diss., New York University, 1973.

5. Council on Interracial Books for Children. *Human and Anti-Human Values in Children's Books.* New York, Council on Interracial Books for Children, 1976.

6. Entwisle, Doris R. "Developmental Sociolinguistics: Inner-City Children." *In* CIBC Racism and Sexism Resource Center for Educators, eds. *Educating the Disadvantaged, School Year 1968-1969.* New York, AMS Press, 1970, vol. 1, pt. 1, pp. 123-36.

7. Soares, Anthony T., and Soares, Louise M. "Self Perceptions of Culturally Disadvantaged Children." *In* CIBC Racism and Sexism Resource Center for Educators, op, cit., pp. 5-19.

MARGARET BUSH
Assistant Professor
School of Library Science
Simmons College
Boston, Massachusetts

Library Facilities for Children, or The Candy-Colored Polyurethane 10-Speed Learning Environment

"How do you like your facilities? What would you like to change? What other things do you wish you had?" If these questions were asked of children's librarians and media specialists, chances are that a few would be wholeheartedly enthusiastic about their working space and its various features. Many others would most likely voice reservations and produce a shopping list.

In preparing this article, the author visited thirteen school libraries and media centers in Boston and children's departments in ten public libraries in eastern Massachusetts and New Hampshire. Personal observation of the facilities and their use by children, coupled with friendly conversation with the people working in the various libraries, was a valuable and fascinating exercise which provided an enormous amount of information.

A few people did like their libraries very much. When asked why this was so, they answered either "It's very attractive, and we have plenty of space," or "We're very pleased with what we've been able to do with the children here." It should be noted that those answers which made immediate rederence to children all came from people who work in a school system where they have had to fight enormous obstacles to establish libraries and media centers. In libraries where people were not so enthusiastic about their facilities, there were three types of responses. The most frequent complaint was a lack of space. The second source of dissatisfaction was the feeling that staff had had no say in planning new or recently expanded buildings. A third — and related — irritation was the fixed nature of unattractive wall graphics or inconvenient structural features which staff could not change. Aside from major problems, all staff tended to wish for very simple things, such as a better paperback rack or a couch for cozier storytelling.

FORM AND FUNCTION

Louis Sullivan's dictum that "form ever follows function"[1] has been cited so often that it bears the familiarity of cliché. Nevertheless, it serves as a useful premise in examining facilities. One thing seems certain: whether form or function has determined the design of a particular building, the environment which is finally created announces the intended function to all who enter. Translated into everyday terms and applied to the individual children's librarian or media specialist, this means that the facility is a reflection of that person's philosophy, policy and objectives. The kind of environment established defines the audience and expresses the librarian's function there.

What form are children's departments taking? In a few extreme cases there are the stone and glass structures, largely devoid of color, which characterize what has been called the "totally designed interior."[2] In this type of building, all aesthetic considerations are determined by the architect. Not all architects anxious to make structural statements are of a stark, symmetrical persuasion, however. Several of the media centers viewed have walls of hard, glossy yellow, orange or red, with bold wall graphics and stairs plunging into the center of the room; some have multilevel areas which created permanent divisions of the available space.

Most library buildings do not follow a bold, unique or extreme design. Usually each develops its own character in some more modest way, but common tendencies appear when any number are compared. These tendencies are worth examining for many reasons: they reveal the prevailing sense of what is aesthetically appropriate for children, and they indicate the services and options available to young library users.

The first and most predominant feature of most children's rooms is the use of color. The old complaints about "institutional green" have been laid to rest. There are new prevailing colors: institutional orange and yellow. Red is also plentiful, occasionally on the walls, and often in furniture and carpets. Turquoise and greens, which psychologists and color experts advise as good choices for libraries[3] appear occasionally as a restful change for the library visitor. Generally, wall tones are muted or sandy hues, while most furniture and equipment are in vivid tones, with deep bright blues, purples and greens joining the reds, yellows and oranges. Many of the common colors have a harsh, bright quality which is especially evident in the acrylic fabrics and plastic and enameled metal furniture that are widely used. These colors are exciting for some library users and disquieting for others. When used in old buildings with dark wood moldings they create a strange sense of disunity.

In American popular culture, plastics and pop art belong to one stream of preference. A separate current of interest runs toward an identification with the natural world. Some libraries do make generous use of brick, natural woods and large windows opening on pleasant outdoor views. This kind of library tends to use color less obtrusively and displays large plants and handsome works of art or crafts. Children's facilities sometimes include generous amounts of plants and may house fish, gerbils or other small animals, but the connection to the natural world is otherwise not much favored. It is apparently believed that the bold and vivid aspects of popular culture with less contrast in tone and texture is more appropriate to the child's world.

Tables and chairs in graduated sizes have long been common features in school and library facilities. Today, the decor and fittings of children's rooms clearly emphasize the library's focus on the young child. Pictures, mobiles, toys and special furniture and play equipment create a very busy atmosphere, one which does not appear to be intended for the older or more serious child. Collection content is broad and varied and generally planned for a wide audience, but the environment may be structured to provide for some activities and users and to neglect others.

THE LEARNING ENVIRONMENT

The rationale for using bright colors and providing many options for busy activity is that such an atmosphere is attractive to children, is exciting, and stimulates learning. Some of these reasons may turn out to be overgeneralizations, and library staff may need to reexamine these assumptions and become more knowledgeable about learning processes (if indeed learning is still seen as a goal of the library). In one library, which had a particularly colorful environment and a large amount of play equipment and molded plastic furniture (much of which had been custom-built by request of the director), the atmosphere seemed charged with the physical energy of children moving excitedly through the room. The staff quietly said that while the children found the environment stimulating, it was virtually impossible to interest them in the use of materials. Good listening equipment was seldom used. Abuse of equipment and furniture was common. The mother of a three-year-old child who had recently moved to the community commented that her son had previously enjoyed selecting his own books at the library, but in this building he was excited and distracted by the activity and equipment and could no longer be bothered with the book collection.

It seems obvious that children's librarians need to examine the ways in which facilities are used and to relate this information to the achievement of goals. Color, design of space and choice of decorative materials and equipment all contribute to the interaction between individuals and their environment.

Psychologists and educators have talked much about color and its importance. The lack of color creates an air of monotony and depresses interest and response on the part of children. Red, orange and yellow are preferred by young children, but these colors draw the attention outward to the environment and create a feeling of excitement which interferes with concentration.[4] These colors work well as points of contrast, but may be less effective on walls and floors. As children grow older, their color preferences become more sophisticated, and they respond well to colors in the blue and green ranges, which are also colors that aid in concentration. People tend to look more pleasant against backgrounds of these colors as well. Choice of color in libraries, then, can be used to stimulate either physical activity, or thought and other imaginative processes. The use of light also relates to color, and librarians have barely begun to explore the variety and control of lighting which might expedite creative programming and use of facilities.

In considering space, librarians are often concerned about the total amount of it or about the space for specific materials, equipment or activities. Another consideration usually neglected is human needs and reactions with regard to space. Some libraries do very well by providing options for division of space; there may be small conference rooms for group study or privacy, open areas where varying arrangements for programs and personal use occur, wired carrels for listening and viewing, formal tables, and informal lounge areas. Other libraries, however, lack imaginative divisions of space, and some violate the need for "private space" (which may occur in open, public places) and the need for quiet study.[5] The terms *work* and *study* seem to be viewed as out of date or inappropriate in a few libraries. Library space today may be very crowded with objects and visual stimuli which bombard the child and which may prevent focusing of attention on any particular thing. The idea seems to be that as many items as possible should be visible.

The variety — and sometimes the similarity — of decor, equipment and materials is fascinating to explore as one visits different libraries. In most of the facilities seen by the writer, the sensory stimuli were all visual or physical. There were plenty of opportunities for listening with record and cassette collections and handy listening stations, but these did not seem to be receiving much use. The notable omission was an appeal to the tactile senses with textural variety. There were a few stuffed animals and small thick-pile scatter rugs. A few libraries had bright-colored foam blocks for seating at programs; staff usually noted that these were very attractive play objects but did not work too well as seating (sometimes less is indeed more, and the floor works better). In the widespread crafts movement today, there is an abundance of woven work, soft sculpture, quilted and appliquéd material, as well as works in clay, glass, wood and basketry[6] that are beautiful, humorous, exciting and largely unexplored in library environments. In four libraries, banners, wall hangings or small quilted pictures were seen. The most interesting craft items on display were large, beautifully constructed papier-mâché figures of Peter Rabbit, Paul Bunyan and a whale.

While libraries are utilizing more audiovisual equipment today, there are still many common machines that can stimulate learning which are not much in evidence. These include typewriters, calculators, magnifying glasses, microscopes, simple drawing mechanisms, and cameras. One unfortunate development has been the widespread increase in vandalism and abuse which librarians are reporting in those places where varied equipment and material have been available. A happier trend is the growing use of puppets in the library, and some very creative work has gone into the design of puppets, stages and productions. Adults are also a part of the regular clientele in the children's rooms, and a parent's corner or collection has become a common feature.

It should be noted that some of the most thoughtful comments on equipment, facilities and environment have been made by writers working in programs for children with physical and learning disabilities. Many of the articles in the recent ALA collection, *The Special Child in the Library,*[7] have broad implications for all people working with children in libraries.

WALLS AND SPACES

Many children's departments are given a very small portion of space in a library building. Others have almost too much space to be manageable by the small staff usually allotted to children's services. Some departments have space that is subdivided into rooms or alcoves. This may facilitate certain kinds of use, but causes traffic and visibility problems. A really good facility requires adequate office, workroom, meeting room or program space in convenient locations. Convenience is also crucial to the location of restroom facilities and telephones. Plumbing and most electrical wiring will be permanent arrangements which are enabling or limiting factors in future use of the building. Plentiful use of phone jacks and movable electrical tracks are important for efficiency and flexibility. Workroom considerations include counter, desk and shelving space, as well as running water and electrical outlets. This room is even more versatile if it can accommodate small groups involved in craft, workshop or simple production techniques.

Major stumbling blocks to flexibility in using and altering facilities are permanent fixtures on walls or built into a room. Wall graphics or murals impose a permanent element into the decor. Shelving or other structures which can never be moved limit future use of the space. Wall surfaces that do not permit the temporary hanging or mounting of art are frustrating. Small rooms and closets, even if fixed in location, can be bonuses, because they can be varied in use. One of the best examples of this was seen in a library where a small conference room had been converted to a periodicals room for children.

Many people dislike a large square or rectangular space for the children's room, and yet this shape often proves to offer the most control and flexibility, since the physical divisions are not permanently fixed. The space can be divided attractively with shelving and furniture, provided that sight lines and traffic flow are carefully considered. Perimeter wall shelving offers many advantages, and walls left free of shelving offer other possibilities for devising storage and display. A common failing in children's rooms continues to be the use of free-standing shelving that is too high for comfortable use by children or that is placed so that it blocks areas from view. This generally contributes to discipline problems and also may cause staff to be unaware of persons needing assistance.

Storage space, both outside of the main service area for children and inside, is of vital importance. Most libraries find it necessary to have some storage provisions that are especially secure for expensive equipment. The great variety of materials in use today requires careful planning of the bins, files, cupboards and cases needed. Often personal ingenuity is called for — this was most evident in school libraries where staff had had the opportunity to attend cardboard carpentry workshops. Cabinets mounted on casters for portability are generally much appreciated.

Children's rooms are most often isolated from the other services and collections of the library, located on a separate floor or in a room closed off to contain traffic and noise. It is expected that all service to children should occur in this separate space, although children's librarians are coming to realize that many children have information needs requiring access to other collections of the library. A concern for providing this kind of access was seldom expressed in the libraries visited. The best traffic flow from one department to another occurred in a building that was 125 years old and consisted of an original wing (which had been a one-room schoolhouse) and two major additions. In this library, the children's librarian was very pleased with the easy movement into adult sections of the library and spoke highly of the teamwork of the staff and constant efforts to make the building and services work better. Staff in other children's departments seemed to appreciate isolation. Several school media centers suffered from a surfeit of accessibility; these had been placed in the center of the school with entry on all sides from class-rooms. A constant stream of traffic passed through the media center to other parts of the building, making staff work with individual students very difficult and communication with groups impossible.

THE PLANNING PROCESS

Complaints that children's librarians are not involved in the planning of new or expanded buildings are difficult for the casual observer to judge fairly. It is clearly evident that in some cases the architect or library direc-tor has used single-minded determination in choosing building design. It was also true in the libraries visited that the most inviting rooms were those in old buildings where library facilities had been improvised and library staff had assumed most of the responsibility for establishing and equipping the space. Personal involvement seems to pay off handsomely.

The political ramifications and technical aspects involved in planning facilities are complex, to say the least. Planning is a process, and if the children's librarian and other staff have not previously been involved in the decision-making and administrative network of the library, it is un-likely they will have much opportunity to participate in the planning of building changes. Many children's librarians need training in strategy to establish their place in the management team. Some are unaware of the need, and some administrators are impervious to their efforts to share decision-making. The effort must be made, however, before major deci-sions are underway.

Wise planning depends on clarity of vision in examining the library's function and goals. Librarians have been skeptical about statistical studies, but they would be better equipped to plan effectively if they be-came acquainted with some techniques involved in user studies and other quantitative measures.[8] They should avail themselves of population studies and projections which may have been done for their geographic area. They could more skillfully deal with facilities if they knew more about the ways in which people interact with their environment. There are some obvious implications here for ongoing personal study and professional education.

CONCLUSION

Planning, some reasonable amount of space, and an enthusiasm for people, materials and ideas, along with some appreciation for aesthetic harmony, are all major ingredients in establishing facilities which are attractive, comfortable and dynamic. Librarians do not know what the future will bring in the way of new materials, services or needs. They do know that they have not begun to live up to their current potential. In some cases, clutter and faddishness have obscured their sense of purpose, and we, as children's librarians, cannot afford this at a time when it is necessary to defend our need for funds. Imagination and courage are needed to try new ideas, evaluate efforts and admit mistakes. Foresight to keep open the opportunity to try again is essential. Some writers have raised exciting possibilities, and some librarians have found creative solutions to space and use problems.

REFERENCES

1. Sullivan, Louis H. "The Tall Office Building Artistically Considered," *Lippincott's Magazine,* March 1896.
2. Von Eckardt, Wolf. "Wolf Von Eckardt on Architecture," *New Republic* 177:32, Aug. 6 & 13, 1977.
3. *See* Birren, Faber. *Light, Color and Environment.* New York, Van Nostrand Reinhold, 1969.
4. Ibid., p. 48; and Thompson, James J. *Beyond Words; Nonverbal Communication in the Classroom.* New York, Citation Press, 1973, p. 71.
5. Ibid., p. 9.
6. West, Virginia. "Fiber Structures at Convergence '76," *Craft Horizons* 36:14-21, Aug. 1976.
7. Baskin, Barbara, and Harris, Karen H., eds. *The Special Child in the Library.* Chicago, ALA, 1976.
8. *See* DeProspo, Ernest R., et al. *Performance Measures for Public Libraries.* Chicago, ALA, 1973.

ADDITIONAL REFERENCES

Holt, Raymond, ed. *An Architectural Strategy for Change; Remodeling and Expanding for Contemporary Public Library Needs*. Chicago, ALA, 1976.

Myller, Rolf. *The Design of the Small Public Library*. New York, R.R. Bowker, 1966.

Schell, Hal B. *Reader on the Library Building*. Englewood, Colo., Microcard Editions Books, 1975.

Tauffner, Gilbert E. "Furniture and Related Facilities to Accommodate Multi-Media Activities in Libraries," *Library Trends* 19:493-507, April 1971.

Ward, Herbert, ed. *New Library Buildings: Architect Librarian Assessments*. London, Library Association, 1974.

Materials

DUDLEY B. CARLSON

Head, Children's Department
Princeton Public Library
Princeton, New Jersey

and

MARGARET MARY KIMMEL

Associate Professor
Graduate School of Library and Information Sciences
University of Pittsburgh

Library Materials for Children

Library materials for children cannot be considered alone, because the term *library* has long implied more than a collection of books. It is fitting that this topic follows papers discussing goals, facilities, staff, services, and children themselves. A collection of materials is a means, not an end.

There is evidence that the isolation of materials from the concept of service is not a new problem. Jesse Shera notes that the development in the nineteenth century of the American public library began with collections of books donated by successful businessmen and philanthropists to uplift the minds of the young. When the Boston Public Library opened its doors in 1854, however, those under eighteen were not admitted. The mere fact that collections of materials for youth existed and had encouraged library development did not mean that children were actually given service.[1] This paper will attempt to raise questions about materials for children in today's public library, their characteristics and availability; and to discuss the relation of materials to other elements of library service.

The sheer volume and variety of materials available to children through libraries presents problems undreamed of by those earlier librarians who had to struggle to develop collections of quality books, established awards to encourage the production of more and better children's books, and trained the children's librarian in the art of storytelling. This volume is due to a proliferation of materials and also to a diversification of clientele. The library is newly aware of potential use by adults, researchers and parents, the special child, the preschooler, and readers and nonreaders of various ages.

Early goals were expressed in terms of a philosophy that viewed the child as an individual needing guidance in reading beyond that received in the classroom. With changes in technology and emphasis shifting away from educational textbooks, however, library collections have expanded to include a greater variety of learning materials, such as toys, games, live animals and plants, uses of which are by no means confined to the classroom or school library. While collections have expanded, statements of goals and directions of service seem to have become more diffuse. Articles proliferate about the purpose or mission of the public library; service to children is not alone in seeking a direction.

In the strictest sense, the object of the collection of children's materials is to provide for a child's information needs, however they are expressed. Patterns of service have developed suggesting that effort be made to do more than that. Librarians try to stimulate and encourage curiosity, to share the excitement of discovery, and to encourage in the child a sense of independence in learning.

But "the times, they are a-changin'," and materials for children are changing — in content, form and style. The information explosion has created a big business, and raises for the children's librarian questions dealing with bibliographic control, availability and reviewing, and their implications for collection development. The absence, in the audiovisual areas, of a comprehensive, up-to-date source of bibliographic citations analogous to *Books in Print* is a significant handicap to the librarian in acquiring children's materials. Records, tapes, films and filmstrips, slides and posters, toys, games, realia — all require careful examination for conceptual as well as technical considerations. The endless search through producers' catalogs and evaluation tools for the sketchiest ordering information is time-consuming and often fruitless. (It is interesting to note that librarians in search of bibliographic data on recordings continue to rely on the *Schwann Catalog,* which is organized to fit the needs of record sales outlets.)

The increasing unavailability of children's books today presents another selection problem of real concern. Old favorites and standard library items disappear from catalogs without warning; brand new titles, given cool receptions, become extinct before proving themselves. The precise status of a book is often difficult to determine, from either the supplier or the publisher. In this framework, the book becomes a commodity whose characteristics are described only in economic terms, without consideration by manufacturer or wholesaler for a thin but nevertheless significant stream of continuing interest. This places on the would-be architect of a well-balanced collection the burden of close scrutiny at time of publication, continuous monitoring of both user interest and publisher availability, and diligent scrounging when a needed title becomes unavailable. It also suggests that both publishers and jobbers should be called to account for their performance in supplying books to libraries, and that children's librarians should research carefully the causes of ambiguous status of books in order to effect change.

If bibliographic data on certain materials are limited, evaluative information is even more so. The librarian who attempts to build a strong collection of records, tapes, filmstrips, etc., must consult a number of sources, only a few of which could be considered comprehensive. The late LeRoy Merritt characterized book reviewing in 1958 as "a chorus of praise, a reluctance to condemn, and a strong tendency to say nothing one way or the other."[2] He might well have been speaking of the field of children's materials today. This failure to be specific or to reflect a point of view is particularly noticeable in the reviewing of nonfiction. Here, a proliferation of titles often occurs within a narrow subject area and it is difficult to find reviews which identify classics or standard titles, mention older books which should be updated or replaced, or list recent titles in the same or similar areas. Such a review would not only provide a more accurate basis for selection but would call attention to the context in which a book may fit.

Furthermore, criteria for reviewers (for any kind of material) are diverse, vague and inconsistent. It is a small world in which librarians, critics, publishers and authors/artists live. We read one another's books, comment on each other's art and sit in judgment on our professional writing. John Hollander, in an essay on the state of the art of reviewing, cited the plight of the poet as a microcosm of the problems of reviewing. One might substitute the field of children's books and professional literature in the following: "Either new books of verse are not reviewed at all, or they are written about by other poets. The result is a lot of mutual taking-in of washing and clique reputation-mongering, all without seeming embarrassment."[3] While it is comforting to talk with a fellow professional, one must guard against introspection which limits one's outlook and merely confirms prejudice.

Closely related to the problems of reviewing is the awkward problem of awards. Questions have been raised about these awards throughout their history, and efforts to refine the process by which they are given continue. New awards have been created in the hope of stimulating growth and improving quality in several nonprint fields, and the procedure for choosing the Newbery and Caldecott Medal winners has recently undergone yet another evolutionary change. It is time for the profession to ask the very basic questions: What purpose do these awards serve today?

Have they become the self-serving tools of either the library profession or the publishing trade?

Furthermore, the conflicting priorities of the reviewer are amplified in awards committees, where literary values must be weighed against social ones, and where the desire for improvement and increased relevance to children vies with artistic integrity and good writing. The time for giving awards may have passed, unless the process by which winners are selected can be made less political and the ends they are to serve more carefully defined. The very fact that such terms as "conflict of interest" and "cronyism" have been directed toward the relationship between awards committee members and publishers of children's books — whether or not such charges are justified — indicates the need to look beyond the details of awards selection and committee procedure. The effects of the awards on children as readers; on adults who buy books; on authors, illustrators, and publishers; and on patterns of children's book publishing and library book purchasing for children must be considered.

The reviewing of materials and problems of bibliographic control have significantly influenced patterns of collection development in the public library. In selecting books, the traditional children's librarian subscribed to a faith in quality typified by De La Mare's "only the rarest kind of best is good enough" and reviewed and debated books in an effort to distinguish good from bad and better from best. This approach, developed and practiced in large municipal systems, has stressed evaluation of the total collection, discussion of current purchases in light of other titles of the same or similar nature, and the need to reexamine long-standing favorites in order to replenish the supply or weed out those titles no longer useful. The significance of such in-house reviewing for staff training and development is sometimes lost on administrators, who hear only the noise of debate and see only expensive duplication of effort in local reviewing.

A different sort of collection development is practiced in those smaller units where selection is done by one or two librarians who rely on instinct, reading-when-possible, and the reviews of one or two journals whose recommendations seem reliable. This is an attempt to acquire the best by eliminating the worst and, together with the method of choosing the best, forms the conventional wisdom disseminated by most library schools.

There are, however, other theories and practices which cannot be ignored. In the Boston Public Library, for instance, one copy of every title published for children in a given year is purchased and made available for branch selection, allowing librarians to build collections that fit the needs of individual communities, without prior selection by a central authority. Emphasis in purchasing is on the current year's production; retrospective replacement lists are generated by subject and are selective.

Another distinctive approach is advocated by the Baltimore County Public Library (BCPL) which drastically limits the number of new titles bought each year and develops collections around patron demand. A study released by the BCPL indicates a commitment "to collecting, not a broad array of materials that librarians feel users *should* read or use, but those materials which most users *do* read or use; to provide these materials as soon after publication as possible; and to support the ensuing demand with sufficient copies to satisfy user requests promptly."[4] This approach, according to Director Charles Robinson, aims at saturating collections with material children want and will read. He contends that it is an underestimation of the library's public to assume that this approach will result only in the mediocre. High circulation figures and increased support from staff and public indicate that the impact of this approach is considerable. The BCPL collection is one that changes constantly. Titles that do not circulate are discarded. While this library's approach to collection development is open to debate, it deserves serious critical attention.

Other policies, not as well articulated and less thoughtful, are practiced far too often. Many collections are not built; they simply grow, with the addition of all the Junior Literary Guild selections, or all prizewinners (regardless of suitability), or whatever the local remainder salesman has on hand. Gifts are accepted without screening; little or no thought is given to selection of titles or to duplication; money is just spent until it runs out.

Collection development is not an end in itself, nor was it invented to occupy the librarian's time. Its object is to provide, as effectively as possible, materials with which to meet user needs. The children's librarian, like any other professional, must know the community in order to assess present and potential needs. Children have changed, perhaps more than librarians who serve them realize. While some of the "Sesame Street" generation have learned to read at an early age, laments are heard at the other end of the educational yardstick about a general decline in the ability of students to read, write and concentrate. Television, combined with other media used by children, seems to have a limiting as well as an expanding effect on the viewer, but little is known about its effect on the learner.

A recent study of children's use of the public library conducted by Adele Fasick and Claire England of the University of Toronto describes those children who use the library as avid television fans. Samples indicate, in fact, that public library users watch as much as nonusers. Watching television does not seem to make the difference between using and not using libraries — even between reading and not reading. Interestingly, both users and nonusers claim to have been encouraged to read because of a television movie, citing such titles as *Heidi, Black Beauty, Anne of Green Gables,* and *Star Trek.* Perhaps one of the most notable facts in this intriguing study is the documented evidence that an overwhelming 87 percent of the children who use the public library are there for books — not programs or even other kinds of materials, although many mentioned an interest in records, games and the like.[5]

One of Fasick's recommendations — that more books of medium quality be added to the collection to encourage library use — strikes a sore spot of many librarians, for here good intentions often become confused with questions of judgment and taste. "Standards of excellence" had been a rallying cry even before Frances Clarke Sayers demanded a belligerent attitude toward the promotion of the best reading for the young. Librarians want to provide the best available books for children, and in searching for the best may overlook the reader who needs plainer fare to help him learn that he can, indeed, enjoy and learn from books, or who needs to approach learning through some other medium before trying the printed word.

Carried to their extremes, problems of selection can lead to the issue of censorship, where theories are posited as truth, charged with emotion and often delivered in raised voices. Dr. Spodek's article on child development and education bears directly on many of the problems of censorship and children. Consider the question of instruction versus information: Do we tell children what they need to know, or show them how to find the information? Does the library provide what children want, or what the librarian believes children need? Should children be exposed only to the positive values adults wish them to emulate, or should children know experiences considered negative as well?

These dilemmas all involve value examination and clarification. We must be willing to face the fact that if we do not buy nonprint materials because we do not like media, we are practicing censorship. If we do not learn about the technology that can give children access to information, we are practicing censorship. If we buy all the prize-winners and none of the less ethereal books that ordinary children ask for, we are practicing censorship. The vague and inconsistent effort to define and refine the complexities of these questions must be resolved. Questions of social responsibility and freedom of access, however, are pervasive and perennial. They cannot be dismissed, but neither can they be allowed to stop everything else.

A collection of materials for children serves many different purposes, but it is necessary to look at the collection in terms of the child's needs and in relation to other materials in the library. For many children, the scope of the children's room, based on criteria related to age, is inadequate when their interests or information needs advance beyond those typical of their age group. The separate children's department exists to meet the special needs of children. The child whose needs have expanded should be expected to pursue his interests in the adult department. Children mature in different areas and at differing rates. While arguments about limiting a child's access to adult materials on any basis other than parental restrictions remain unconvincing, it is the children's librarian who bears responsibility for guidance of a child.

Like adults, children seeking information are frequently unaware of the variety of resources available to them. Without avoiding the public library's responsibility for providing information, the children's librarian should become familiar with and introduce children to other local sources of information, such as museums, historical or cultural societies, and even government records. As in any adult department, a community resource file to which patrons may be referred is important. First among such resources is the child's own school library.

Clearly, school/public library cooperation is not a new concept, but it is a logical first step in broadening a child's access. A recent study in New Mexico, for instance, indicates that virtually all the hardware and equipment exists in public schools, while software is housed in the public library.[6] It may be that cooperation between types of libraries is difficult in some jurisdictions, but there is evidence that even small libraries can support interlibrary loan networks. A study done by Ellen Altman indicates that interlibrary loan is feasible in a sample of public secondary school libraries; at least 48 percent of the collections in the sampled secondary schools were unique titles, and 31.4 percent of the school titles were not held in the public library. The study concluded that the collections in the schools are diversified and could support an interlibrary loan network.[7] There does not seem to be a corresponding survey of the diversity of public library collections, but if collection building methods served as indicators, diversity would definitely be "statistically significant."

Collections of children's materials also serve the needs of parents, teachers, scout leaders, artists, adults with reading problems and others concerned with children and their development. The Fasick study found that 20 percent of the circulation of children's materials in the Regina Public Library System was to adults.[8] This is another aspect of collection development that needs consideration as adult education programs studying the literature proliferate. Master's degree programs are now underway (or soon will be) at several colleges, and at least one major university offers a Ph.D. in children's literature. Planners of children's services have always been aware of the adult working with or interested in children, but the scholar or researcher has not always been considered, and the problems are significant.

The researcher is interested not only in the history of children's books, but in all aspects of child life: family, play and welfare. Furthermore, when dealing with contemporary books, the student wants both the good and the not-so-good. The student is interested in the poor writing, the stilted dialogue, and the trite plot precisely because of the need to study what makes a good (or bad) book. Educational institutions must support their own teaching activities, of course; these teaching collections will have to present the controversial, the less than perfect, the "trendy" literature for the very reason that the public library has rejected these books. Titles reflecting racial or sexual stereotypes, slanted or biased points of view, slick distortion, and so on must be available to the student somewhere.

The trend toward extensive resource-sharing among libraries serving adults has broad implications for service to children, many of which remain largely unexplored. These concepts have been the subject of conferences, papers, books — and most especially the concern of the National Commission on Libraries and Information Science (NCLIS). The NCLIS reports as one of its goals for action: "To eventually provide every individual in the United States with equal opportunity of access to that part of the total information resource which will satisfy the individual's educational, working, cultural and leisure-time needs and interest, regardless of the individual's location, social or physical condition or level of intellectual achievement."[9] The phrase "regardless of . . . level of intellectual achievement" might lead one to believe that children and their requests are welcomed, that the ability to pursue an interest beyond the scope of the local library is encouraged and that the child is able to find additional titles by a favorite author. For children, however, access to such information is often severely limited, sometimes by the reluctance of library personnel to accept a child's request as serious or legitimate, but often by limitations built into the system itself. In New Jersey, for instance, libraries are encouraged to request children's books throughout the New Jersey library network. Local libraries may submit juvenile requests to their own area libraries, which, in turn, refer unfilled requests to the state library. Some area libraries will undertake lateral searches among libraries in the region; others do not. If, however, the state library's collection does not contain the title sought, the manual on interlibrary loan procedures states that "juvenile in-print titles . . . should *not* be requested," having been proscribed with "ephemeral fic-

tion, current 'best sellers,' titles announced in current alerting tools . . .
and titles available in mass-market editions."[10] Furthermore, requests
for titles published after 1956 may not be made to the Pennsylvania Union
Catalog (PUC), with which New Jersey has a contract covering "some
4,000,000 titles, reported by some 200 Pennsylvania libraries."[11] (PUC's
juvenile additions stopped in 1956.)

Although library systems and networks may in fact practice resource-
sharing within their own jurisdictions, the development of resource-sharing across political and geographic boundaries remains outside the scope
of most service to children and beyond the priority considerations of many
children's librarians. A number of areas of consideration invite further
exploration:

1. *Sharing collections on a trial basis* — In many areas financial restrictions severely limit the individual library's freedom to experiment
   with new or controversial materials. Through cooperative efforts of
   several libraries, development, utilization and evaluation of collections of toys and games, special audiovisual materials or equipment
   or other such materials could be developed. Such an alliance might
   represent school and public libraries within a limited geographic area,
   as well as members of regional systems, or be offered through state
   library agencies.
2. *Children's materials for adults* — The importance of developing special collections of materials for adults has been stressed by ALSC's
   Committee on National Planning of Special Collections and others.[12]
   Cooperation between public libraries, and colleges and universities
   offering courses in children's literature, offers an intriguing opportunity for cooperative planning in collection development.
3. *Media examination centers* — This is not a new concept by any means,
   but is one which needs to be developed for coherent collection development, especially for the smaller, independent or rural public
   library or school where there is often no available resource for examination of a broad range of children's materials.

The structure and method of resource-sharing and interlibrary loan networks for children's material is debatable. The need for such access is not.

A fighting posture or even goodwill on the part of librarians will not
assure that access. There must be participation in the planning and development of interlibrary loan schemes and on-line bibliographic retrieval
systems. NCLIS has appointed a task force on the "Role of the School
Library Media Program in Networking," but the group has no one representing children's services in public libraries. This is another example of
the fragmentation of power of those who are concerned about children.

When the New York Commissioner's report about combining public and school library service to children was issued in 1970, public and school people united only in the horror of the moment and then retreated to their pinnacled institutions to defend what was and had been. If a child's right to information is to be developed and enlarged, if children's literature is to be critically studied, a system of networking which commits the sin of omission cannot be allowed to develop.

We have moved very quickly from *Peter Rabbit* to on-line data bases — and some librarians don't like it. An administrator of a public library recently noted that one children's librarian's response to a query about selection procedures was "But you'll take all the fun out of being a children's librarian." Problems of management and implications of restrictive access for children do not make the job less challenging. These questions open up new possibilities. Colleagues who discuss career opportunities with new professionals may recommend the field instead of suggesting anything *but* children's work, because the opportunities are too limited. By relating goals for service to thoughtful, creative collections of materials, library service to children should be able to grow and develop with the same enthusiasm, zest and optimism that characterize the children to be served.

REFERENCES

1. Shera, Jesse H. *Foundations of the Public Library: The Origins of the Public Library Movement in New England, 1629-1855*. Hamden, Conn., Shoe String Press, 1974.

2. Merritt, LeRoy, et al. *Reviews in Library Book Selection*. Detroit, Wayne State University Press, 1958, p. 39.

3. Hollander, John. "Some Animadversions on Current Reviewing." *In* Roger Smith, ed. *The American Reading Public: What It Reads, Why It Reads*. New York, R.R. Bowker, 1963, p. 227.

4. Palmour, Vernon E., and Bellassai, Marcia. *To Satisfy Demand: A Study Plan for Public Library Service in Baltimore County*. Arlington, Va., Center for Naval Analysis, Public Research Institute, 1977.

5. Fasick, Adele, and England, Claire. *Children Using Media: Reading and Viewing Preferences Among the Users and Non-Users of the Regina Public Library*. (Prepared by the Centre for Research in Librarianship, Faculty of Library Science, University of Toronto.) Toronto, Centre for Research in Librarianship, University of Toronto, 1977.

6. Gillentine, Jane, and Roberts, Jim. *New Mexico State Library Film Services: A Study With Recommendations*. Santa Fe, New Mexico State Library, 1974.

7. Altman, Ellen. "The Resource Capabilities of Public Secondary School Libraries to Support Interlibrary Loan: A Systems Approach to Title Diversity and Collection Overlap." Ph.D. diss., Graduate Library School, Rutgers University, 1971.

8. Fasick and England, op. cit., p. 3.

9. National Commission on Libraries and Information Science. *Toward a National Program for Library and Information Services: Goals for Action.* Washington, D.C., U.S.G.P.O., 1975, p. xi.

10. New Jersey State Department of Education. Interlibrary Reference and Loan Service. *Interlibrary Loan, Photocopy and Reference Procedures Manual.* Trenton, N.J., Department of Education, 1973, p. 19.

11. Ibid., p. 20.

12. *See, for example,* Henne, Frances. "Toward a National Plan to Nourish Research in Children's Literature," *Wilson Library Bulletin* 50:131-37, Oct. 1975.

MARY E. KINGSBURY
Associate Professor
School of Library Science
University of North Carolina at Chapel Hill

Keeping Out of Trouble: Research and Children's Services of Public Libraries

The nineteenth-century humorist, Artemus Ward, once said: "It ain't the things we don't know that get us in trouble. It's the things we know that ain't so." That pithy statement sums up the value of research to the library profession. Good research can help to keep us out of trouble; it brings respectability to a profession. However, as members of a profession not noted for the quality or even the quantity of its research, librarians would do well to worry less about achieving respectability and concentrate more on finding out what they need to know to keep out of trouble.

Twenty years ago Frances Henne called for a systematic program of research. "Thus far," she wrote, "many, if not most, of the problems in the area of library work with youth have not been explored objectively, and many principles, standards and procedures commonly accepted and practiced have never been tested or evaluated."[1] If, during the past twenty years, librarians had systematically and objectively evaluated what they were doing, would they be in the trouble they are today?

Librarians concerned with services to children face two alternatives. They can opt to defend the status quo and the practices that support it, nourishing professional myths, passing them on to new recruits and ignoring the fact that some of them are now paraprofessionals rather than librarians. To remain on that course, however, is unrealistic. Those who elect to keep their feet on the ground, rocky though it may be, must reject the temporary comforts of the status quo and, as Fagin put it in the film *Oliver,* must begin "to reevaluate the situation."

Therein lies the value of research. It can help dispel the visions of unreality. Moreover, research findings can win support; the force of evidence is often necessary to convince people of the value of children's services. The problem to date is that children's librarians have had no facts — lots of feelings, but no facts. As the political scientist Kenneth Beasley warned ten years ago, "developing library service in terms of intuition . . . is an anachronism that must be recognized at once."[2] How much truer that is today, when it borders on recklessness to expect those responsible for disbursing funds to accede to one's intuitions about services to children! Librarians must argue with facts, not feelings; hence the need for research to get them out of trouble and to keep them out.

What is meant by research? Most of the research in librarianship, like the social sciences, has been nonexperimental. Many of the research problems in librarianship, for example, simply do not lend themselves to experimental research methods, in which an attempt is made to control all the variables. However, they do lend themselves to the systematic and objective study called for in the research methods employed in the social sciences. Librarians need not simply be content with the myriad descriptive reports of successful programs in individual libraries that make up so much of the professional literature.

Perhaps this tendency to confuse research with these subjective descriptions of narrow or merely local problems comes from a limited acquaintance with research methodologies. The cautious researcher sticks with a known technique, allowing it to determine the problem to be studied. Hans Selye tells of a young researcher who developed a procedure for determining the amount of fecal iron in rats. He spent the remainder of his career asking people on campus if they were running any experiments in which accurate determinations of the amount of fecal iron in rats would be useful.[3] Considering this, it seems that one of the obstacles to truly productive research is the propensity for selecting topics that lend themselves to familiar research methods. This leads some people to become positively Pickwickian in their concentration on manageable topics. The profession would be better served, and the time of the researcher better spent, if consideration were given first to the choice of a pressing problem that calls for research and then to the research design and appropriate methodologies.

Contributors to the professional literature of a more masochistic bent enjoy harping on the fact that library science has never produced a unique method of research and must borrow from other disciplines. Comfort can be found in the words of the American philosopher, Charles Peirce, who wrote that "the higher places in science in the coming years are for those who succeed in adapting the methods of one science to the investigation of another. . . ."⁴ Librarians don't need to flagellate themselves because they as a profession have not developed their own research methodologies. If the day ever comes when all the possibilities of methodologies developed by other disciplines have been exhausted, librarians will be forced to innovate. In the meantime, there is an array of approaches to select from in the event that a problem needs to be solved or a curiosity wants to be satisfied.

The library profession's finest efforts to date, for example, may be the historical studies that have been completed. And although they didn't invent content analysis, they have certainly profited from it. Citation analysis as well as methods of literary research that might be borrowed from the humanists can also be used to study materials for children.

A less familiar methodology, one practically synonymous with anthropology, is participant observation. Anthropologists are using participant observation in field studies in the United States. Increasingly, studies are being carried out in urban settings. An anthropologist recently published an ethnography on the person in the principal's office, the result of participant observation in an elementary school.⁵ Why not an ethnography on a children's librarian? The children's room in a public library would make an ideal field for such a study.

Survey research offers one of the richest methodological lodes, one that the library science profession has barely begun to tap. Kerlinger uses the term *scientific* survey research to differentiate it from status surveys,⁶ with which everyone is familiar. Salary surveys are an example of this. Such studies are directed at determining the status quo, not at studying relations among variables. Their importance is in bringing together large quantities of data that can be compared over the years. Survey research, on the other hand, seeks to determine what people think and what they do. Sociological variables, such as age, sex, race, education, and political affiliation, are related to psychological variables, such as opinions, attitudes and behavior. A number of methods are used to gather such information: personal interviews, mail questionnaires, telephone interviews, panels, and controlled observation. A schedule or questionnaire is used to organize the gathering of information.

Most methods of survey research have been developed by psychologists, sociologists, economists, political scientists, anthropologists, and statisticians. It might be consoling to know that the rigorous scientific aspects of survey research that have greatly influenced the social sciences developed after World War II with the refinement in sampling procedures. In another twenty-five years librarianship, too, may be approaching scientific elegance and rigor.

Quite frankly, the reason for the emphasis on social science research methods, particularly survey research, is the personal conviction that this is the kind of research that children's services needs most. The best content analysis in the world multiplied by 100 will not convince a skeptical library director to support children's services as much as will a piece of survey research demonstrating that the taxpayers in the community place services to children at the top of their list of library priorities. Before pointing up areas in need of study, it seems appropriate to review some of the more recent research relating to services and materials for children.

Reviewing recent research points to the conclusion that more work has been done relating to materials than to any other aspect of children's services. Monson and Peltola in their annotated bibliography, *Research in Children's Literature,*[7] contrast the period 1960-65, in which only twenty-three dissertations related to children's literature were cited in *Dissertation Abstracts International,* with the single year 1971, in which thirty-one were cited. Their bibliography covers the period 1960-74 and includes dissertations, ERIC studies, journal articles, and related studies such as books, monographs and library school master's degree theses.

So extensive has the research on children's literature become that there is now an excellent journal, *Phaedrus,* devoted to maintaining bibliographic control of the current research. *Phaedrus* provides coverage of journal articles based on research, although it does exclude more readily accessible journals such as *The Horn Book* and *Children's Literature in Education. Phaedrus,* together with the Monson bibliography and Lukenbill's *A Working Bibliography of American Doctoral Dissertations in Children's and Adolescents' Literature, 1930-1971,*[8] provides control of dissertation research since 1930. *Library Literature* also lists dissertations completed in library schools and some master's level research, making control of research on children's literature fairly complete.

Content analysis is the research methodology favored by those who want to move beyond the subjective evaluation of children's books to an objective analysis of the content of a systematically selected sample of books, films, etc. It shifts the study of the content of children's materials away from the murky realm of opinion and into the revealing spotlight of critical analysis. If carried out in a scientific manner, it is terribly time-consuming. It does, however, offer the advantage of being manageable; a doctoral student willing to invest the time can be certain of completing a dissertation while enjoying some good reading or viewing along the way. There is no waiting for respondents to return survey instruments, no need to send follow-up letters, no worry that the return rate will be unacceptable. Obviously, content analysis has much to recommend it as a methodology well suited to the study of library materials. One might go so far as to say that anyone interested in library research should have more than a passing familiarity with this technique.

A cursory look at the topics treated in recent studies reveals a focus ranging from the cozy "Rabbits in Children's Books" to the controversial "Violence in Realistic Fiction for Children," with continued attention to topics of current interest. Many articles purporting to be content analyses are merely casual examinations of the content of a small number of books that either happened to be at hand or contained themes the writer was looking for. The sweeping generalizations made in such articles often seem in indirect proportion to the weight of the evidence. In sharp contrast to such superficial efforts, Mary Lou Green completed a dissertation in 1975 using thirteen categories to analyze ninety books that included a death theme.[9]

Finally, the whole area of sexism in children's books is now being given systematic study. A dissertation by Harriet Fraad explored the sex-role stereotyping in several categories of children's picture books printed between 1959 and 1972: best-selling Golden Books, *New York Times* best-sellers, Caldecott Medal books, sex-role picture books, and women's liberation children's books.[10] The instrument used was a checklist of thirty-three research-based male and female sex-role standards. Not surprisingly, one finding was that male characters were in the majority in all except the women's liberation books throughout the entire period.

William F. Whyte once recommended that the training of young sociologists shift from an emphasis on covering the literature (which in large measure, he claimed, merely documents ignorance) toward providing students the tools for finding things out for themselves.[11] A systematic coverage of the literature reporting research on children's services leads to the conclusion that either there is no ignorance to document, or librarians are too smart to reveal it by publication. A computer search of a number of data bases (ERIC, *Social Science Citation Index, Dissertation Abstracts* and *Psych Abstracts*) and a manual search of the leading journals in sociology, anthropology and political science revealed that research relating to public libraries is scarce and research related to children's services even more so. As Marian Gallivan points out in her annotated bibliography on research in children's services,[12] much more research has been done on school libraries than on public libraries. In locating research projects published from 1960 through fall 1972, she found thirty-two studies on school libraries and only fourteen on public libraries. That average of about one per year is maintained by the six studies reported here.

Some insight into the characteristics of users and nonusers of public library services for children comes from a 1972 dissertation completed at the University of Washington by Myriette R.G. Ekechukwu.[13] A pretested questionnaire was sent to 472 fifth-graders in 19 elementary schools. Results disclosed a significant relationship between use and nonuse and attitudes toward the public library. Not surprisingly, a greater number of fifth-graders were school library users than public library users. The percentage of fifth-graders with favorable attitudes toward public libraries was greater, however, than the percentage of users with favorable attitudes toward school libraries. The book collection was the aspect that fifth-graders liked best about public and school libraries; the rules and regulations were the most disliked element. The major reason for use of both libraries was to borrow books to read outside the library. Use of library materials for school-related purposes was the second most frequently-mentioned reason for use of both libraries.

Jean Tower studied changes in children's library services for selected Pittsburgh suburbs in relation to changes in that population for 1960 through 1970.[14] Data were collected through interviews with staff working with young children in twenty-five public and school libraries. Findings revealed that the quality of children's library service improved markedly as the population rose. In each element (resources, staff and budgets), school libraries showed greater change than public libraries. Tower noted that this reflected Pennsylvania's mandate of school library programs and the fact that Elementary and Secondary Education Act Title II funds were far larger than those available to public libraries through Title I of the Library Services and Construction Act.

Blanche Woolls focused on cooperative library services to children in public libraries and public school systems in selected communities in Indiana.[15] The population chosen for the study was 24 communities having: (1) a population of 5000 or more; (2) a public library and elementary schools; and (3) children's librarians, school librarians, school library supervisors or any combination of the three. Questionnaires were completed in fall 1972 by 53 librarians and 2473 fifth-grade children in randomly selected schools and classrooms. Results showed that access to a school library did not terminate use of the public library; 7 percent went to the public library more than once a week, 13 percent once a month. Findings revealed little cooperation; program planning was not a shared activity of school and public librarians. In determining which staffing pattern facilitated the most cooperation and communication, Woolls found that the greatest amount of communication and cooperative activities existed in a small city that had no children's librarian in the public library but did have school librarians and a school library supervisor. Of the librarians surveyed, 7 percent rated working relations between public libraries and school libraries as poor, 31 percent fair, 35 percent good, and 15 percent excellent.

The last three studies to be reported represent a sampling of opinion on the national level. In spring 1975, coordinators of children's services in the fifty largest U.S. cities were asked by this writer to suggest one or two goals, trends and/or innovations likely to be present in children's services in the public libraries over the last quarter-century, and also to provide the name of a well-qualified children's librarian. Sixty-two percent (thirty-one) responded to this request. Their suggestions, reduced to a manageable number of goal, trend and innovation statements, were then sent back as a questionnaire to all fifty coordinators and to the recommended librarians. Sixty-five percent of the total group returned the completed questionnaire; 62 percent (thirty coordinators and twenty librarians) returned it in time to be included in the final results.

The findings on the trends foreseen by the respondents appear in the report from the Detroit preconference[16] and the findings on the goals established in the study have been published in the January 1978 issue of *School Library Journal,* so there is no need to repeat them here. Of the suggested innovations, the one that respondents would most like to see introduced into library practice is to have library directors and other administrators realize that children's librarians who have been in the forefront in employing outreach techniques, interagency cooperation, new media, etc., have the potential to provide leadership for the entire library. Someday library historians will acknowledge that children's librarians were ahead of their colleagues in initiating such practices, but it seems ironic that recognition is so difficult to win from one's contemporaries. Perhaps it is a case of the prophet without honor; be that as it may, it is an innovation whose time, one hopes, will come in the not-too-distant future.

Esther Dyer completed a dissertation at Columbia in 1976 in which she used the Delphi methodology to investigate alternative cooperative patterns in library services to children.[17] Completing the study were 130 persons: 16 library directors, 21 children's coordinators, 20 library educators, 18 school superintendents, 17 media supervisors, 20 state consultants, and 18 nationwide experts (individuals concerned with planning or publishing on a nationwide basis). Dyer's panelists judged the probability and the desirability of occurrence of seventy-four potential events on two 5-point scales. The events, developed from literature searches, other forecasts and interviews with experts, concerned financing, organization, administration, staffing and facilities for library services to children during the next fifteen years. Events on which members did not reach consensus were returned for reconsideration. Consensus was generally defined as a two-thirds agreement of a panel as to an event's occurrence. It is interesting to note that only 14.5 percent made any changes in their original evaluations.

Dyer's report of results touched on four major points of interest: the survival of services to children, the desirability of cooperation, the preferred means of coordination, and the probable areas of successful cooperative programs. The essential question, as Dyer points out, involves the survival of public library services to children. The future appears uncertain for urban public libraries; 42 percent of all panelists forecast a decline, but only 14 percent indicate the probability of total elimination of children's services. Library directors are least optimistic: 63 percent believe a decline will take place in the next fifteen years, although only 6 percent believe children's services will be eliminated.

Turning to the question of cooperation between school and public libraries, Dyer reported that respondents judged cooperative efforts to be more desirable than probable, but did suggest that a lack of financial support and outside pressures may force school and public libraries to cooperate. Dyer summarizes her study by characterizing it as a "refresher course in institutional rigidity" and notes that the highest priorities for both institutions are "self-preservation and protection of territory."[18] Cooperation is viewed as an implicit threat to autonomy and, as such, stands little chance of being implemented in the next fifteen years.

In June 1977, Mae Benne of the University of Washington completed the data-gathering phase for a project partially funded by the Library Resources Council[19] which may well become a landmark study in the history of children's services in public libraries. Her 80-page monograph has just been published by the School of Librarianship at the University of Washington. The objectives of the study were: (1) to identify the roles and functions of the central children's library as performed in twenty-seven urban library systems in the United States and two in Canada; and (2) to determine how these functions had been affected by changes in the central city, by changes in administrative patterns, and by priorities set in response to financial problems affecting large urban centers.

In the selection of libraries, Benne attempted to include only urban centers with a population ranking in the first fifty cities. (Actually, the twenty-seven American cities chosen rank among the first thirty-three.) Other factors were: (1) regional representation, (2) history of children's services from the central library, (3) administrative changes affecting children's services or the central children's library, (4) changes in the central city, and (5) budget reductions forcing the establishment of priorities.

A few observations shared by Benne at the Detroit preconference suggest that her monograph will be required reading for all concerned with children's services. In those libraries able to offer Sunday hours, she reported, several found that more than one-half the circulation from the children's collection occurs on weekends. Not surprisingly, slightly more than one-half of the systems reported a decrease in the number of professional positions for children's librarians. In a few libraries, the qualifications of persons filling such jobs have also changed. In one library with over thirty children's staff positions, two-thirds of the occupants lack the MLS degree.

Benne observed that she associates the word *isolation* with the thought of the central children's library. Only twenty of the twenty-eight central libraries that hold departmental meetings require the children's librarians to attend. In some situations, the children's coordinator represents the children's librarian; in others, both attend. In four libraries, however, no member of the children's staff participates. In only seventeen of the twenty-six central libraries using committees to carry on library business do children's librarians assume committee responsibilities. Regardless of any personal feelings about the burden of committee work, this is still an appalling statistic. Benne's study represents the most recent research on children's services and brings up the consideration of future research needs.

Thinking about areas for further research makes one feel a bit like Little Jack Horner with his Christmas pie — putting in a thumb anywhere will pull out a plum of needed research. One place to consider beginning a study on children's materials is the fifth edition of Sutherland and Arbuthnot's *Children and Books*[20] in which Dorothy Broderick and her colleagues offer numerous suggestions for researchable topics.

At last summer's ALA meeting, the Research and Development Committee of ALSC discussed a number of research needs contributed by committee member Ann Pellowski, who gave permission to include them in this paper. Pellowski stated that the following kinds of information were almost totally lacking in available and documented sources:

1. The cost of delivery of children's library service, especially in relation to delivery of other types of services to children.
2. The impact of alternative forms of library service to children on a controlled set of several groups of children. By alternative forms of library service is meant not only the school/public library types, but alternative forms within each one.
3. The reading interests of children, and how they are influenced or affected by limited availability, maximum availability, promotional activities, etc.

4. The training of children's librarians or specialists in children's services. How effective do present administrators believe it to be? The practicing children's librarians themselves?

Participants at the Detroit preconference repeatedly voiced the need for measuring the cost-effectiveness of library services for children; five of the eight discussion groups called on the profession to develop new ways to determine the effectiveness of library service to children. Not enough research has been done on any aspect of children's services and materials, but one area that has been covered relates to children's literature — studies of content and reading interests. This is not to denigrate studies of the literature. It is merely to point out that what is desperately needed today is not more analysis of the content of this much-loved literature, but rather some hard facts about the effectiveness of the services provided to children in public libraries of all sizes and in all geographic and economic areas. What is needed is a national study.

Most are familiar with the expression, "Think big and paint an elephant." Think for a moment about painting an elephant — figuratively speaking, that is. Would it not be possible to bring together a team of researchers and librarians representing all regions of the country who, over a summer perhaps, could design a national study of the effectiveness of children's services? Calling in an outside consultant skilled in research design and questionnaire construction would probably save time and money. The use of a national polling organization such as Lou Harris or Gallup, although expensive, would result in a better study. In place of Harris pollsters, a citizens' group such as the League of Women Voters could conduct the survey. It might even be possible to include a few questions about libraries in general and children's services in particular; this would not cost as much as using a separate instrument. By starting with the concept of a national study that will produce an instrument also usable at the local level, shouldn't it be possible to get some financial support from libraries across the nation? Certainly, most public libraries could come up with about fifty dollars, if for that small amount of money they received a questionnaire that could be used in their communities. Nor does it seem unreasonable to expect that a study designed to determine the effectiveness of children's services would be worth a few thousand dollars in support from ALSC and PLA. This is a sketchy outline, but it does suggest the feasibility of a national study.

The need for library systems to involve the community in assessing what the library's contribution should be was discussed at the Detroit preconference, and mention has been made here of involving children in determining and evaluating services. Libraries can achieve this community involvement through two research approaches that are gaining attention in the social sciences, particularly in political science. The first approach, one that has developed primarily at the federal level, is policy research. The purpose of social policy research is to search systematically for information that can contribute to better social policies. In making a decision that affects library policy, for example, five tasks are usually performed: clarification of goals, description of trends, analysis of conditions, projection of future developments, and evaluation of alternatives. Policy research is especially concerned with studying the effects of alternative policies. If, as seems evident, decisions about library services qualify as social policies, then it follows that library planners can profit from greater knowledge of policy research. Policy research would get libraries into the active search for both community input in planning library service and community feedback for evaluating the effects of existing or newly-initiated services.

A second approach is research which is directed at determining community priorities for the allocation of scarce resources, such as money, land, energy, time, etc. Political scientists have developed a priorities game that would be an excellent means of finding out exactly how members of the community, including children, would allocate money and time for various library services.[21] The game requires the use of interviewers, but again it should be possible to use trained community volunteers.

The whole problem of national priorities is being mentioned more frequently in the media. Establishing priorities for the allocation of human and monetary resources is a challenge that confronts every administrator from the President of the United States to the director of the nation's smallest public library. Too often, the priorities simply reflect the whims of the particular administrator rather than the needs and desires of the institution's public. It would clearly be more practical to have concrete evidence to guide such allocations — evidence that priorities research can provide. Moreover, in addition to a national study of the effectiveness of library services, it would be more than useful to do a national priorities study. It is not rash to think that a study of the priorities for library service held by the people of this country would find services to children at the top of the list. Such a national study could be replicated on the local level if library directors denied the validity of the national findings for their respective libraries.

There are several reasons why there is a paucity of research in the field of librarianship. Writers cite various impediments to research: administrative duties, routine teaching of elementary courses, interruptions due to poor planning of the daily agenda, money, personnel, and even fear. A few seem more prevalent in library science than in other professions and disciplines, and especially prevalent in children's services. Obstacles such as the lack of human models and the difficulties of getting research published are not insurmountable, but they may tend to deter the faint of heart.

To whom does the neophyte researcher look for inspiration today? Not many names come to mind from the ranks of the library profession in general, or from the ranks of those involved in children's work in particular. The tyro about to launch out into the uncharted sea of research in children's services cannot expect to find many guiding lights to mark the reefs and shoals. This alone is enough to make some turn back to shore. Imagine, however, a veritable Ged determined to sail to the farthest shore of the sea of research. The project is designed, the data are gathered; now comes one of the greatest obstacles to completed research — writing it up. Gilbert Highet, in his small classic *The Art of Teaching,*[22] relates a story of the physicist Rutherford, who criticized the habit that some have of spending months collecting data and then begrudging the hours necessary to write it up. One rarely meets anyone engaged in research who finds writing up the findings as interesting as collecting the data. Nevertheless, the refusal to write for publication means that the findings will never be disseminated to the profession at large.

This brings up the problem of finding a place to publish research reports. Very few library publications are much interested in children's services, and the few that are often seem reluctant to publish a research report with its tables and statistics. Most of them prefer a chatty article in which the research findings are reduced to narrative form. I refuse to think that editors want a simplified article because they don't think their readers are intelligent enough to understand a research report. The success of the Research Forums put on by AASL and ALSC clearly indicates that members of these subgroups are just as interested in research as are members of the Library Research Round Table. Be that as it may, the fact that the researcher knows there are limited outlets for research can be a deterrent. Those concerned with children's services in public libraries do not, for example, have their own journal, as do their colleagues serving children in the schools.

Solving this most pressing problem, the determination of the effectiveness of children's services, will not be impossible. Conferences and preconferences, however, are not the solution. Talk about the need to justify services is cheap and easy; actually to design ways to do it will not be. Research, and that is what is needed, is seldom cheap and rarely easy. What research doesn't cost in dollars, it costs in time of those devoted to doing it.

Who is responsible to the profession for conducting this kind of research? The responsibility, it seems, lies with library educators who have as their professional obligation not only teaching, but also the advancement of knowledge. Those who are members of university faculties are paid not just to teach, but also to do research. In his essay "Universities and Their Function," Alfred North Whitehead speaks of universities as "schools of education, and schools of research," and says that a good test for the general efficiency of a faculty is the quality of its publications.[23] Doing research while teaching full-time often means working nights and weekends, but that is part of a university professorship.

A number of years ago, Leon Carnovsky pointed out that library schools should be taking the lead in library investigations and that the profession should look to them for solutions.[24] In the same vein, Maurice Tauber stated that "library school faculties, particularly those associated with institutions having advanced or doctoral programs, have a special responsibility for the development of integrated programs of research."[25] It has always been a personal source of wonder how library school faculties can train candidates adequately for the Ph.D. — a research degree — when the faculty members themselves are not actively engaged in research. Perhaps the criticism which those in their ivory towers receive from the real world might be mitigated if practitioners were able to profit from some of the research educators are supposedly doing. To provide the practitioners with usable research findings seems to be exactly the kind of public service that those with research degrees, in the research environment offered by any university worth the name, and with the specific charge to do research, can best offer to the profession.

Pauline Wilson, in an article on barriers to research that every library school faculty member should read from time to time, cites excessive participation in professional organizations as one barrier to research productivity.[26] This is not to say that faculty from library schools should not be active in their professional organizations but, as Wilson concludes, if an activity can be done equally well by a practitioner, it probably should be. Justice Brandeis once said that what is needed for achievement is brains, time, rectitude, and singleness of purpose. The opportunities offered by higher offices in the professional organizations use up both the time and the singleness of purpose essential to successful research. Those serving in universities have the additional obligation to further the university's traditional role as critic of society. How is it possible to serve as critics of professional organizations, for example, while serving as their administrators? To repeat, if an activity can be done equally well by a practitioner, it should be. Let those from the universities provide leadership in research, but followership in professional organizations.

This is not a ploy to ensure that educators will be left in peace in the ivory tower. I recently completed a questionnaire for some fellow evidently gathering data for his dissertation. One section asked to rank various activities according to their value in helping the respondent stay current with teaching responsibilities. I gave the highest ranking to only two activities — reading professional literature and research. Actually doing research, particularly that of national scope, is the single best means of gaining an overview of the trends in the profession.

If research is so valuable to the individual, why don't more people engage in it? Fear of failure may be one answer. Seriously, those starting out on a career of research need all the encouragement they can get. Completing a dissertation does not qualify a person as a researcher; it is merely a license to practice. A friend once said that he had been practicing medicine for nearly two years before he had the courage to do an appendectomy. While starting a research project is not equivalent to cutting into someone's belly, it does take courage and discipline. Perhaps fear coupled with natural inertia is a near-fatal combination that keeps many from moving out of the comfortable area of teaching into the much less predictable area of research. It is difficult, for example, to be a poor teacher of children's literature. The materials are so good that the students will profit from the course in spite of possible flaws in the professor. However, it is not difficult to be a poor researcher. The challenge is to stay with the process long enough to become competent. Hippocrates said of medicine that "life is short, the art is long, opportunity fleeting, experiment dangerous and judgment difficult." His words apply as well to research.

New Ph.D.s entering the ranks of university faculty may have to screw their courage to the sticking point if they want to survive. Those seeking appointments in university faculties today find an entirely different environment from that prevailing in the 1960s. There may be an overabundance of library science faculty yet, but once appointed to a position, the untenured professor faces much more difficulty getting tenure than in the past. Today, in an increasing number of universities, the faculty member seeking promotion and tenure must not only meet library school standards (which may still be low because of the presence of faculty who got tenure without having done research), but must also pass muster at higher university levels. On these university-wide committees sit professors from traditionally research-oriented departments. There is reason in this for optimism about the future of research in librarianship. The fear of not securing tenure may be sufficiently strong to overcome the fear of starting research. The blighted academic job market may well start a research tradition in library science. Research is habit-forming; the more one does, the more one wants to do.

The problem will be to direct these newly-motivated energies into productive research that will benefit children's services — and that calls for cooperation from practitioners. Although the research buck stops here — in front of the library educators in the universities — practitioners have the obligation to bring to academic attention the problems that need research. These needs might be channeled through ALSC's Research and Development Committee, which could then serve as a sort of Saturday market to which doctoral students searching for a manageable dissertation topic (or the new Ph.D. about to begin the first research beyond the dissertation) could turn for suggestions. This stop-and-shop idea may offend the research purists who hold to the ideal view of research for its own sake. Because this is a field that so desperately needs research, however, there is nothing wrong with trying to bring together researchers and research topics. The plan should be viewed as promoting not shotgun marriages, but merely some marriage of convenience.

Comparing research to marriage has some historical precedent. Richard Altick, in *The Scholar Adventurers,* quotes a seventeenth-century nobleman who described scholarly curiosity as giving pleasure like that of wrestling with a fine woman.[27] Later writers have refined that sexist comment, comparing research to a love affair or marriage. Who knows, another Alex Comfort may be about to make publishing history with *The Joy of Research.* For all is not burdensome and tedious; some joys do accrue to those who seek the adventure of the mind known as the research process. In an article entitled "Pity the Library School Teacher," Haynes McMullen says that library science faculty deserve pity if they do not spend a large portion of their time in research.[28] Wanting others to know one's findings leads to another joy — establishing collegial relationships. A mail survey, for example, leads to the fun of finding a full mailbox and never needing to feel like Charlie Brown. There also comes the satisfaction (after the absolute misery) of knowing that a particular methodological mistake will never be made again. Above all is the pleasure of satisfying personal curiosity; research is like scratching where it itches.

Robert Browning's dramatic poem, "Paracelsus," presents the hero as a man obsessed with an aspiration to discover the secret of the world. Paracelsus sets out in spite of the dissuasion of his friends, Festus and Michael. His farewell to them expresses exactly the courage and resoluteness required of those who abandon themselves to the certain frustrations and the uncertain joys of research.

Are there not, Festus, are there not, dear Michael,
Two points in the adventure of the diver,
One — when, a beggar, he prepares to plunge,
One — when, a prince, he rises with his pearl?
Festus, I plunge![29]

It is to be hoped that in the years ahead, many researchers investigating children's services in public libraries will rise with findings that will prove more valuable than pearls to the profession.

REFERENCES

1. Henne, Frances. "The Frontiers of Library Service for Youth." *In* Frances Henne, et al., eds. *Youth, Communication and Libraries.* Chicago, ALA, 1949, pp. 221-22.

2. Beasley, Kenneth E. "A Theoretical Framework for Public Library Measurement." *In* Herbert Goldhor, ed. *Research Methods in Librarianship: Measurement and Evaluation.* Urbana, University of Illinois Graduate School of Library Science, 1968, p. 12.

3. Selye, Hans. *From Dream to Discovery.* New York, Arno, 1975.

4. Peirce, Charles S. *Selected Writings — Values in a Universe of Change.* New York, Dover Press, 1958, p. 337.

5. Wolcott, Harry F. *The Man in the Principal's Office; An Ethnography.* New York, Holt, Rinehart and Winston, 1973.

6. Kerlinger, Fred N. *Foundations of Behavioral Research.* New York, Holt, Rinehart and Winston, 1964, pp. 394-95.

7. Monson, Dianne L., and Peltola, Bette J., eds. *Research in Children's Literature.* Newark, Delaware, International Reading Association, 1976.

8. Lukenbill, W. Bernard. *A Working Bibliography of American Doctoral Dissertations in Children's and Adolescents' Literature, 1930-1971.* Urbana, University of Illinois Graduate School of Library Science, 1972.

9. Green, Mary Lou J. "The Image of Death as Portrayed in Fiction for Children." Ed.D. diss., Lehigh University, 1975.

10. Fraad, Harriet. "Sex-Role Stereotyping and Male-Female Character Distribution in Popular, Prestigious, and Sex-Role Defining Children's Literature from 1959 to 1972." Ed.D. diss., Columbia University Teachers College, 1975.

11. Whyte, William F. "Reflections on My Work." *In* Mary Lee Bundy and Paul Wasserman, eds. *Reader in Research Methods for Librarianship.* Washington, D.C., NCR Microcard Editions, 1970, p. 316.

12. Gallivan, Marian F. "Research on Children's Services in Libraries," *Top of the News* 30:275-93, April 1974.

13. Ekechukwu, Myriette R.G. "Characteristics of Users and Non-users of Elementary School Library Services and Public Library Services for Children." Ph.D. diss., University of Washington, 1972.

14. Tower, Jean D. "A Study of Changes in Children's Library Services for Selected Pittsburgh Suburbs Related to Their Population for 1960 through 1970." Ph.D. diss., University of Pittsburgh, 1972.

15. Woolls, E. Blanche. "Cooperative Library Services to Children in Public Libraries and Public School Systems in Selected Communities in Indiana." Ph.D. diss., Indiana University, 1973.

16. "The Changing Role in Children's Work in Public Libraries; Issues and Answers." Detroit, Detroit Public Library, 1977.

17. Dyer, Esther R. "New Perspective in Cooperation in Library Service to Children," *School Media Quarterly* 5:261-70, Summer 1977.

18. Ibid., p. 270.

19. Benne, Mae. *The Central Children's Library in Metropolitan Public Libraries.* Seattle, School of Librarianship, University of Washington, 1977.

20. Sutherland, Zena, and Arbuthnot, May H. *Children and Books.* 5th ed. Glenview, Ill., Scott, Foresman, 1977.

21. Beardsley, Philip L., et al. *Measuring Public Opinion on National Priorities: A Report on a Pilot Study.* Beverly Hills, Sage Publications, 1974.

22. Highet, Gilbert. *The Art of Teaching.* New York, Knopf, 1954, p. 210.

23. Whitehead, Alfred North. *The Aims of Education and Other Essays.* New York, Macmillan, 1929, p. 138.

24. Carnovsky, Leon. "Publishing the Results of Research in Librarianship," *Library Trends* 13:126-40, July 1964.

25. Tauber, Maurice F. "Introduction," *Library Trends* 6:108, Oct. 1957.

26. Wilson, Pauline. "Barriers to Research in Library Schools: A Framework for Analysis," *Journal of Education for Librarianship* 17:3-19, Summer 1976.

27. Altick, Richard. *The Scholar Adventurers.* New York, Macmillan, 1950.

28. McMullen, Haynes. "Pity the Library School Teacher," *Library Journal* 89:2280-84, June 1, 1964.

29. Browning, Robert. "Paracelsus." In *The Works of Robert Browning.* New York, Barnes & Noble, 1966, vol. 1, p. 64.

BONNIE S. FOWLER

Head, Children's Dept.
Forsyth County Public Library
Winston-Salem, North Carolina

Reactions by a Recent Library School Graduate

For some of you it has probably been quite a few years since you began as professional librarians, for others it may have been only a few years, but for me it has been exactly ten months and five days since I began work as a professional librarian. Despite the facts that I had worked at my public library part-time for five years before attending library school, and that I had been well-trained for some aspects of my work, there were other aspects of my new position for which I was not so well prepared. Forsyth County has a population of approximately 250,000 and I am the only professional children's librarian in a traditional public library setting. I head the children's department in the main library where, with two other children's room staff members, we maintain collections of children's books, records and art prints, as well as plan and conduct regular programming. Our department also houses a beehive and a long-haired Peruvian guinea pig named Popcorn. Although I do not direct children's programming in the branches, I am often called on for guidance by the branch librarians. Thus, I am not only responsible for children's services at the main library, but am also in part responsible for children's programming at our eight branch libraries.

With such responsibilities, I have faced many difficulties in my first year. One of my difficulties was becoming acquainted with my patrons and their needs. I realized that if I were to select materials and plan programs for the public, I first had to know the public. I had to learn when they would come to the library for programs and for what kind of services they would come. Even more difficult, I had to learn the differences between short- and long-term needs. Another trouble I encountered was in budgeting my time. While I had many time-consuming administrative duties, I had to allow time to serve the public. Although I wanted to at times, I could not barricade myself in my office away from the public. I wanted to spend some time working with my young patrons. Therefore, I have had to learn, and am still learning, to schedule priorities and to budget my time and energy accordingly.

Next were the problems of planning services and of evaluating them afterward. Both of these I knew should be done, but they have often been hard to do. I have had to learn to plan in detail and with a time schedule to ensure that everything would be done properly and on time. In evaluating our services, I have come to realize that I must write some very practical objectives and evaluate services according to them. Finally, I have to mention the many troubles I have encountered in working with people — how to prove myself to those doubtful of my abilities, how to motivate my coworkers when plans have gone astray, how to promote children's services to other people both inside and outside of the library setting. These challenges, in addition to those mentioned earlier, have all contributed to a most interesting and eventful year.

Thus, I looked to the Allerton institute as a refresher course to answer some of my new questions and to remind me of things that I had forgotten. I was not quite sure what to expect, for although the speakers and their subjects seemed impressive, I feared that I might not be able to relate their ideas to my own situation. Therefore, I came with hope, and with some anxiety that my hopes might not be fulfilled. Based on this background, I shall give you some of my impressions of this institute.

One of my first impressions was of the people. When I arrived, I noticed how varied a group we are, men and women of all ages from all over the nation. Coming from large and small libraries, from many aspects of library work, we vary in background and in experience, yet we all have something in common — we are all interested in library work for children. I was immediately impressed with the enthusiasm that I saw. Everywhere I looked, I saw people sharing ideas with each other. I saw old friends renewing acquaintances and new friendships being formed. I heard people discussing the strengths of their services as well as the problems they encounter. I heard how other librarians have faced the same practical difficulties that I have, and we exchanged ideas about our own solutions. By talking with others, I began to understand better my own library system and its strengths and weaknesses. I also realized that the scheduled speakers were not the only ones at this conference to share their knowledge. Everyone had the opportunity both to teach and to learn.

Another impression, developed during the opening session of the conference, was one of amazement at the wealth of knowledge and dedication that we have had presented to us by our speakers. We must thank the planning committee for the incredible feat of bringing together so many notable people to share their ideas and studies with us. They have spoken with an authority which I, for one, respect, and they have given us a blend of the philosophical and the practical, the paragon and the real. Furthermore, unlike other conferences where speakers must rush off to other meetings, our speakers were here much of the time that they were not on the program. This made them available for questions, elaborations — and sometimes debate about their presentations.

The subjects covered during this conference were so varied that there must truly have been something for every children's librarian. However, I do have a few criticisms which I feel should be expressed. First, I wish we could have heard something about school libraries, perhaps the public library children's librarian as viewed by the school librarian. We hear much about the necessity of relating public library children's services to school library services, and I wished to have something about this included. Next, I felt the need for more discussion time as a group. The brochure for this institute said we all were to be given the opportunity "to express, probe and reflect upon viewpoints," and I must admit that occasionally, participant reaction seemed to be stifled. Of course, time limitation and the size of the group made it difficult for group discussion, but it might have been better anticipated and planned for. Finally, and this one is not too critical, I must admit to being somewhat disappointed that in the services section, no one addressed the problems of the library system of the size I am associated with. I know it is there somewhere between medium and large systems, but neither group would claim it.

Getting away from these criticisms, I want to comment on an idea which was repeatedly mentioned at the conference — the idea of cooperation. Certainly this is not a new idea to children's librarians, but it can be a problematic one. Librarians must work with many different groups of people, so the idea of cooperation is an important one. I want to share with you a few of the first steps in cooperation we are taking in North Carolina. In my work I have tried to foster the true spirit of cooperation of which Bridget Lamont spoke; I ask "What can I do for you?" For the most part, my experiences have been pleasant and fruitful. Within my library, I promote this idea by making available to other departments the services of my children's department staff. I have encouraged my staff to serve on interdepartmental committees and to remember that the children's department is only one of many facets of library service. We have also tried to include other departments in our own programs and services.

Recently, we had a storytelling festival to which we invited members of the staff who were not then working with children but who had done some storytelling in the past.

In North Carolina, we also have a very well-organized means of communication with other public children's librarians. We are trying to overcome our isolation. Every three months our state consultant for public library work with children meets in five different areas of the state with the public children's librarians of that area. At our meetings, we preview new books, films and other library materials. There is a time for us to share our programming ideas and other news, and to hear a speech about some aspect of library work. Each time the meeting is in a different library, and often librarians with special skills, such as flannel-board storytelling, are encouraged to share that skill by performing for the group. These meetings are always very helpful and informative.

Some other important forms of cooperation are those between public librarians and school librarians, and those between public librarians and teachers. Here again, I stress the importance of reaching these groups through the positive approach of what the public library can do for them, rather than what they might do for the public library. Public and school librarians might easily cooperate on programming. While public librarians often have the time to plan programs, they do not have ready access to large numbers of children, as school librarians do. On the other hand, school librarians often do not have the time to plan programs. Perhaps in some cases, the public library could present some of its well-planned programs for the school library's children. For teachers, the public librarians might provide orientation programs to library materials and services. In our school system, all of the schools have coordinators who head the reading programs in their respective school. I have been to the monthly meetings of these coordinators to tell them about new materials and upcoming programs. They in turn have told teachers in their schools, and our library has received many calls for materials and services from these teachers. Cooperation with these groups has helped our library, and although my steps have been small and slow, I feel that they have been important.

In closing, I would like to say one more thing about this Allerton institute. For me, it has been a needed retreat from my day-to-day library life. Although I enjoy my work, it has been, as I have said, a difficult first year. I have had to learn many practical things which could not be taught in any library school. I have had to face the problems of selection and programming that all librarians must face. This retreat has given me the opportunity to rest from my daily worries and to evaluate what I have done in the past year. It has reminded me that long-range goals cannot and really should not be achieved quickly, and that the steps toward these goals must be carefully planned and articulated. I have also been given the chance to evaluate myself as a children's librarian, to acknowledge my talents and skills, and to recognize areas which need development or change. Tomorrow I will return to my library with a fresher spirit than when I left. Certainly not all of my questions have been answered, but I have gained insight and confidence from my experience here at the Allerton institute. I hope you, too, will return to your libraries with a renewed spirit for and a clearer understanding of our profession. I also hope that the Allerton institute will not end here, but that you will carry the ideas expressed here to your fellow professionals who have not attended. The Allerton institute has reminded us all of what public library work for children can and should be.

MILDRED L. BATCHELDER
Retired Executive Secretary
Children's Services Division
American Library Association
Chicago, Illinois

Reactions by a Retired Leader

From the viewpoint of a beginning librarian who is ten months into a promising career to that of a retired librarian more than ten years beyond a professional lifetime's involvement with library services to children is quite a distance. That decade has involved few contacts with libraries for me. Instead, I have been learning the pleasures and problems of volunteerism, working with the Evanston Historical Society, the League of Women Voters and several conservation projects. This institute has been highly stimulating — an opportunity to see old friends and to become acquainted with a cross-section of currently active children's librarians. Here, as in my children's services days, I find the personal contacts most rewarding.

Because of my years away from library service, I expected the institute to reveal changes in libraries and in services to children. However, I was quite unprepared for the extent of those changes. Let me take library provision of audiovisual materials as an example. In 1942 ALA published a book on educational films and libraries.[1] I was involved in this activity as the ALA staff contact with the Visual Methods Committee, later called the Audio-Visual Committee. We had to search to find the few libraries whose programs were reported. ALA encouraged library involvement with films and recordings, but public library recognition of responsibility for these materials was slow in coming. Present-day librarians can scarcely imagine the lack of library interest in these materials then. School librarians were more reponsive because there was more local pressure on them to use audiovisual materials. Companies selling projectors and other equipment carried on elaborate and successful campaigns to persuade school administrators that the machines, although expensive, were essential. There was no such promotion to introduce to the public library the valuable information and experience in film which these machines would make accessible. Librarians felt threatened by the machines and their introduction to film materials was discouragingly limited. All of this was only twenty-five or thirty years ago; things are very different today. Every talk, every conversation, takes for granted library responsibility for all types of communication materials — not only audiovisual. There is even, I have learned, some extraordinary library provision of toys.

More astonishing to me is the extent of library use of communications technology. Data banks, computers, extensive union catalogs that do or do not include children's books — these are things which had not touched me a dozen years ago. Of course, some librarians concerned with research were already exploring and using these instruments, but if any children's librarians were then using them in relation to children's books and services, they were indeed in the vanguard. Clearly, the products of these technologies can do and are doing marvelous things for libraries, including children's services. I sense that some librarians feel uncertain, perhaps fearful and ignorant of what those possibilities are. Is it essential to learn about those possibilities? This is an area in which children's librarians must not permit themselves to be labeled as isolationist. They must become aware of the possibilities and act if children's services are to benefit.

As far as politics are concerned, I do not know how librarians learn their roles in the political life of the community and state. Early in my career I traveled with two librarians who were masters of the art. The elected officials and the librarians knew each other well and were skillful in working together. Each had respect for the other. At this institute I have heard several comments which indicate a nervousness or uncertainty about the children's librarian's relationship to politics. Obviously, the library administrator holds the forefront in this relationship, but surely the entire staff — and especially the children's librarians — must see themselves as part of a team working together for basic library effectiveness. It is not enough to work at politics only when a library referendum is in the offing.

The references to new, well-planned uses of volunteers delight me. Hospitals have made fine use of volunteers for years. Most hospitals carefully determine appropriate activities for volunteers and have worked out training programs which clarify what volunteers do and what is done by professionals. Use of young people as volunteers in work with children is an idea which seems to have double value. The idea of volunteers for providing programs has excellent potential and it was good to hear the warning that the library must develop a philosophy for library programs which must be understood and adhered to by the volunteers. Older persons could be used as volunteers in libraries; I have seen news stories about foster grandparents. Some older persons enjoy being with children and, if there are no grandchildren or nearby neighbor children, they might appreciate opportunities to help with children in libraries.

Library services to parents seem to be very well established, especially for parents of preschool children. However, the question has been raised whether parents of school-age children, especially of middle-school children, are served as consistently and well as the parents of preschoolers. That is worth thinking about and examining.

One of the great changes over this 10-year period seems to be in services to handicapped children, and not only to the blind and deaf children who have been served to some extent by libraries for many years. Through government funds to libraries and other organizations in the communities, library services have been greatly and imaginatively extended to large numbers of children unreached before. Serving them is splendid and in doing so, every effort must be made to provide that service in such a way that the children feel themselves to be just children — not handicapped children. As a person considered by some to be handicapped because I use two canes, I know how important it is to feel regular, not special.

Concerning children with severe problems and the value which books may have for them, I would like to mention the article "Cushla," published in *Signal,* a British magazine on children's books.[2] Cushla is a very ill child whose problem-fraught life is immensely aided by books read to her and shared with her from the age of four months to nearly four years old. The article lists the books and her age when they were used, commenting on her responses as time went on. Among the results was Cushla's quite unusual knowledge of words. Real experiences were necessarily limited, but book experiences had given her a vocabulary which must surely have made her slip into reading herself quite easily. Perhaps we should think about tripling or quadrupling our expenditures for books for infants and very young children, and possibly include funds for toys. Help for parents in the use of books and toys would be important in such a program.

The materials sessions most assuredly brought up ideas that will be around for some time. Much thought, much discussion, some confusion, agreements, disagreements and, gradually, new directions will presumably emerge. It is high time for these discussions, and the discussions along the way are going to be as fruitful as the positions finally reached.

Similarly, the goals presentation did not repeat the past literature on the subject. It will serve as a base for starting discussions locally and at state and national meetings. Best results will come from the rethinking and perhaps remolding by each children's librarian of her own goals.

Frequent reference has been made to the paragon that children's librarians are expected to be if they are to accomplish all that is recommended. Problems in working with administrators were referred to often. The facts that children's services must be recognized as an integral part of the library's service, and that children's librarians must involve themselves and be involved by the administrator in the goals and activities of the entire library were also mentioned. A very practical answer to improving relations with administrators is widespread membership and active participation of children's librarians in the Public Library Association. Perhaps children's librarians themselves are to blame if they are labeled isolationists. Perhaps it is our fault if we have problems with our administrators. The $15 it costs an ALSC member to join PLA can be the most important investment in success in this profession. I would like to see 50 percent of the children's librarians in ALSC become PLA members in 1978.

REFERENCES

1. McDonald, Gerald D. *Educational Motion Pictures and Libraries*. Chicago, ALA, 1942.

2. Butler, Dorothy. "Cushla," *Signal*, No. 22, Jan. 1977, pp. 3-37. *See also* Lowe, Virginia. "Cushla, Carol and Rebecca," *Signal*, No. 24, Sept. 1977, pp. 140-48.

CAROL N. EULLER
Library Media Specialist
Webster Central School
Webster, New York

Reactions by a School Librarian

It may appear strange to a group of public library children's librarians to have a school librarian in their midst; however, elementary school librarians are children's librarians, too, and I am delighted that the planners of the institute share this view. I admit that I love my job, but do not love all children; liking children and liking to work with them in a library is what is important. My favorite professional colleagues have always been public children's librarians and the ALA involvement that has brought me the greatest satisfaction has been with the Association for Library Service to Children (ALSC). Therefore, to be included at this institute discussing children's services of public libraries seems very fitting.

I have tried to pinpoint problems mentioned at this institute that are common to both school and public libraries. Some concerns were brought up by more than one speaker. Peggy Sullivan referred to the isolation of the children's librarian. Mary Jane Anderson pointed out the geographical isolation (except for those in urban areas) of children's librarians. I submit that school librarians are even more in isolation. They neither work in a building with another librarian nor under an administrator with a background in librarianship. The solution for both school and public librarians appears to be simple. Every suburban branch is surrounded by several elementary school libraries. Why are there seldom, if ever, mutual meetings, mutual exchanges, sharing of mutual concerns? Why are we not united in our communities, sharing goals and solving problems together? Why does a feeling of noncooperation exist? Surely it is not because the issue of public and school cooperation has never been dealt with in the literature. As long ago as 1948, ALA published *A National Plan for Public Library Service*[1] advocating the development of a formula to meet this need. As recently as summer 1977, the research findings of Esther R. Dyer were published in *School Media Quarterly*.[2] Dyer's discouraging conclusion is that both public and school librarians are "shut . . . up in a tower of cooperative virtue,"[3] powerless to bring about cooperation while busily blaming one another for its lack. We appear to be motivated — or not motivated, depending on your point of view — by the fear that each of us will lose our autonomy.

There are other current issues that encourage cooperation. Mainstreaming of the handicapped and the need that this long-overdue movement creates for special skills and materials is one. The passage of this federal law has not brought a stampede to our doors, but the time to be ready is before, not after, the first arrival. The special needs of gifted children is another. Such children are difficult to identify without sharing the results of testing and observation in the schools. Canney also reminded us in his presentation that the very important preschool years prepare children for learning to read. School librarians are not aware of the extent to which we depend on the public librarian to make this preparation before the children enter kindergarten. We need to be told and to share our knowledge of the reading process with you.

Media selection as a problem for the less media-experienced public children's librarians was mentioned by both Barbara Rollock and Bridget Lamont. School librarians are nonprint media specialists by necessity. Most school media centers on the elementary level have at minimum a collection of filmstrips, cassette tapes and disk recordings; some also have 8mm loop films, microfiche and videotapes, and the equipment for their use, much of which the children may borrow for home use. District-wide preview and evaluation procedures screen new materials before purchase. This information must be shared if limited budgets are to be spent wisely and the best material provided for our patrons.

Zero population growth (ZPG) is a cause I support in spite of the fact that it was probably a factor in the closing last June of the 14-year-old school in which I had served as sole librarian from its beginning. I left there a library created into a model media center through an ESEA Title II grant, predominantly green (the color Margaret Bush described as most desirable for children's libraries) and having the recommended conference room, large workroom for projects, private places, and complete visibility. How the closing of schools all over the country will affect children's services in public libraries is not entirely clear, but it certainly must follow that for many children, the public library and not the school library, will become geographically the nearest library to their homes.

Barbara Rollock reminded us of the New York State Commissioner of Education's Committee on Library Development which, in the early part of this decade, recommended that all services to children, preschool through grade six, be the responsibility of the elementary school media centers. A task force drew up guidelines for a pilot project. Shortly before this conference, I received a letter from Lore Scurrah,[4] Chief of the New York State Bureau of School Libraries, stating that because of a continuing lack of funds, plans for the pilot project had been shelved and would not be resubmitted. Had the pilot been successful and in favor of the recommendation, children's rooms might no longer exist in New York State today.

Scurrah referred to a new project for her department — networking, a heated topic at this conference. Elementary school librarians in general would be surprised at this, for some are just beginning to recognize its implications. Perhaps that is part of the reason for the present situation that excludes children's materials in resource-sharing. We need public children's librarians to wake us up and we need to work together toward equal rights for children.

The spirited discussions on access to materials have caused me to reflect on how access is restricted or influenced in a school. The right of access to an adult collection does not exist, but we restrict children in other ways. Some of these are tendencies shared with public children's librarians, others are not:

1. the librarian who selects or does not select;
2. the principal who sets school policy;
3. the nurse-teacher who does not want the children to read sex books before she teaches them the unit;
4. the reading teacher who wants the child to have books only on his or her reading level;
5. the classroom teacher who does not want children to borrow Christmas books in October;
6. the parent who wants to deny a book to all students; and
7. the custodian who reports when the librarian weeds the collection.

Slashed budgets and staff cuts have also been mentioned. School librarians are familiar with this problem, too. A clerical assistant is a staff member unknown to most elementary school librarians. We work alone, except for volunteers (usually mothers of pupils) whose intent is commendable but whose usefulness is questionable. While prices go up, budgets for libraries and schools go down.

Librarians are often criticized for talking about books too much at meetings rather than talking about children and services. If this is so, how can it be that for the past four days, none of the children's librarians here has referred to the fact that this week is Children's Book Week?

REFERENCES

1. Joeckel, Carleton B., and Winslow, Amy. *A National Plan for Public Library Service*. Chicago, ALA, 1948, p. 93.

2. Dyer, Esther R. "New Perspective on Cooperation in Library Services to Children," *School Media Quarterly*, 5:261-70, Summer 1977.

3. Ibid., p. 269.

4. Scurrah, Lore. Personal communication, Oct. 20, 1977.

ALEXANDER W. TODD, JR.
Director
Fountaindale Public Library District
Bolingbrook, Illinois

Reactions by a Public Library Administrator

I must confess that I came to this institute expecting dry dissertations on the ivory-tower level that would have a sedative effect on me — in short, an opportunity to rest my weary director bones and catch up on a little napping. What a rude awakening! The speakers, participants and agenda have kept me interested and alert — perhaps because they were reinforcing my beliefs.

Peggy Sullivan began by asking if children's librarians are sure that they have goals for public library service for children. A good question — and after three days, there has been no answer. Or, if the goals exist, you surely don't know how to state them. Bernard Spodek made the point that libraries are not schools, but are arenas for mental action. Keep this in mind: libraries are not a replacement for formal education. George Canney reinforced this premise by emphasizing that librarians do not teach reading.

To Spencer Shaw's comments, I say, hallelujah! A children's librarian should have knowledge of the total environment, knowledge of children and their world, and most of all, knowledge of organization of services, management skills and the philosophy connected with library service to children. Carolyn Field has shown from her presentation that she is first and foremost a librarian, and secondarily one who specializes in children's services. William Chait's observations are accurate; librarians must experiment and develop rapport with both children and adults. Librarians must develop adult interests within themselves. Norma

Rogers points out that children are individuals with individual tastes, who want well-informed librarians, not book-checkers. Thanks should be expressed to Faith Hektoen and Mary Jane Anderson for stating that librarians must know the content and impact of library materials, and that to grow, the librarian must break out of the local setting by joining and becoming active in professional organizations.

At this point, a spirited discussion took place that astounded me as a director. I heard administrators described as parsimonious, perverse, pigheaded, intolerant, aloof, unsympathetic and outright nasty ogres who regularly discriminate against children's librarians and their programs. Would you care to wager that the same would be said at a meeting of adult services librarians, or that a meeting of technical services librarians would agree with you, too?

I submit that we, the enemy, are really reasonable individuals who will react positively *if* you do your homework, know what you want, why you want it, what it will do for library service as a whole, what you need to do it, what it will cost in both time and dollars, and what will be the inevitable reaction to your proposal. Present this in a logical and orderly manner and you have an excellent chance of getting what you want. Remember, you must convince only one person — that person must convince a board of seven or more. Give the boss complete background work so his or her job will be easier. However, be careful; you may get what you ask for! To keep administrators happy, keep them advised of activities on a regular basis. Ask questions. Communicate! Have the courage of your convictions. Educate the director. A well-informed boss will have a greater tendency to try to accommodate your desires, plans and programs. If you don't think you're getting a fair deal, look at yourself first.

Bridget Lamont made the point that children's librarians like to talk only among themselves and then wonder why no one takes them seriously. Beating-a-dead-horse syndrome, perhaps? Amy Kellman prescribed the three purposes of programs: increase library visibility, bring people in, and stimulate use of library materials. Barbara Rollock accurately stated that librarians are not social workers.

Environment (i.e., facilities) is essential to positive service, according to Margaret Bush. I might add, though, that it is not a substitute for a friendly, well-informed and dynamic librarian.

Margaret Kimmel and Dudley Carlson asked who is responsible for materials selection. The answer is the administrator, who then delegates responsibility to departmental librarians. Selectors should give readers what they want, not what selectors think is good for them. Adult selectors should not ignore Emily Loring, Grace Livingston Hill, and the nurse stories because they are poor literature. Why do too many children's librarians opt not to clutter their shelves with the Hardy Boys, Nancy Drew or, heaven forbid, the Bobbsey Twins? I say if you do have these, they won't clutter your shelves — they will be out most of the time. Try it and see. Most of your so-called lasting literature will last, and last, and last . . . because it is never used.

Mary Kingsbury leads into an interesting point with her statistic from the Benne study that "in one library with over thirty children's staff positions, two-thirds of the occupants lack the MLS." In recruiting for librarians to staff two new libraries in the past two years, I have found that the graduate library schools appear to emphasize training and coursework for: first, academic librarianship; second, special librarianship; third, media specialists; fourth, public librarianship; and fifth — if you can't do anything else — children's librarianship. Very few of the resumes I received indicated "service to children" as the primary job objective, and the coursework taken seemed to back this up. I am glad to learn from Spencer Shaw that the University of Washington is correcting this curriculum oversight. More schools should follow this lead.

What is the future of children's services? Let me use songs from three Broadway musicals to illustrate:

"Baubles, Bangles and Beads" from *Kismet* — follow this philosophy of service through crafts, games and fun times only, and your future is dim;

"Impossible Dream" from *Man of La Mancha* — follow the high ideals of trying to be all things to all people without regard for reality and practicality — tilt with windmills, if you will — and your future is even dimmer and rather short-lived;

"You Gotta Know the Territory" (the theme of the lead song "Rock Island") from *Music Man* — apply the philosophy of a salesman: know the product, know the customer, know the territory. You are selling a product and have stiff competition from the park district, television, school programs and other forms of recreation. To sell your unique product, you must advertise. You must create a congenial atmosphere. You must know your job. You must stop keeping your light under a bushel basket and let administrators know what you are doing and plan to do. You must develop managerial skills in supervision, budgeting and planning. When you want something, ask directly and apply the six ps: Proper prior planning prevents poor performance. Do all this and stop feeling sorry for yourself because you are "just children's librarians" and you will blossom and flourish, grow and command respect . . . and higher salaries . . . and have a bright and limitless future. The future is yours — what you do with it is up to you.

Evaluations of the Institute Program

HERBERT GOLDHOR

Director
Graduate School of Library Science
University of Illinois
Urbana-Champaign

Summary

This has been a very worthwhile institute, and it is now my task to summarize what has been said here. For a number of years I was a public librarian but never a children's librarian; I am greatly interested in children's work, however, and over the years have known a number of children's librarians reasonably well. I do not claim any special knowledge or insights into this field, and if I happen to say anything which is particularly apt or strikes home, it is probably by chance and not design.

What I say here constitutes my views of what I think I heard and sometimes what I listened for and did not hear. That is to say, this is not an objective or factual summary of what each speaker said but rather my own perceptions of some of the main themes which were developed here. When I speak of books, I mean to include under that term all media.

I have organized my remarks in the form of several generalizations or guiding principles, without significance to the order of listing. First, it is clear that children's work in public libraries has had a long and distinguished history, has attracted many outstanding people, and has made many important contributions. These latter include: (1) creating the climate for school libraries; (2) always searching for new groups of patrons to serve, e.g., preschool children, the handicapped and outreach service to children of immigrant, minority and disadvantaged groups; (3) developing new services and activities, e.g., the story hour, the summer reading club, puppet shows, creative writing clubs, etc.; (4) influencing publishers to produce more and better books for children; and (5) pioneering in library use of nonprint, audiovisual materials. In fact, the early literature of librarianship makes mention of most activities which are conducted or being considered today; for example, the Youngstown (Ohio) Public Library had a parents' room before 1920.

Great and glorious as the past has been, children's librarians cannot expect to be allowed to rest on their laurels. Society and the world tend always to ask, "But what have you done for us lately?" To justify their work, children's librarians must continue to make contributions, to adapt to new and changing circumstances, and to find good solutions to new problems, as well as ever-better solutions to old problems.

Second, children's work in public libraries has long faced a number of major problems. School librarians are in a sense allies of the public library children's department, but in another sense they are competitors. They are much better supported than children's work has ever been, for both materials and staff, and they no longer restrict themselves to curricular materials only but seek to encompass the recreational and general reading interests of children. The great increase in children's books over the years and the rise of new media, along with an ever-wider span of children's interests, have made book selection much more difficult, not to speak of shrinking revenues and rising costs. Children's librarians generally feel that they lack the support they need from public library directors. For example, children's librarians feel that they get a small part of the library's budget in proportion to their contribution to the library's total service program; and they feel that they are generally not involved in planning even the future of children's work, let alone that of the library generally.

In 1964 the "Index of American Public Library Circulation" showed a record high (since 1939) of 52 percent juvenile circulation of total public library loans. Since then juvenile circulation has dropped steadily to 32 percent in 1976, while total public library circulation has gone up 20 percent. For better or worse, the one standard measure of use which we have is circulation, and by this measure children's work has been declining.

Third, it is necessary to state clearly what seems to have been implied by various speakers, i.e., that children's work in public libraries is important for its own sake and not simply or mainly in order to inculcate the library habit or to raise up a generation of adult library users. Children's librarians many years ago used to advance those latter arguments as justifying support for their work, but the evidence does not support that point of view. Library service to children is important and desirable in its own right, because children need, want and use books and libraries. To judge from Spodek's presentation, we don't know for sure how children learn and mature, and thus how they can best be helped; but we librarians are convinced that books and reading are necessary elements in that process.

In fact, as we all know, children and books go together naturally, joyously and with good results. In part this may be because books serve children as a substitute for real life; the young child cannot safely experience directly many things which older children and adults can. From five to nine years of age, almost all children use books and libraries heavily, if they have the chance; from ten to fourteen years of age, somewhat fewer children are readers and public library patrons; in high school, even fewer; and in early adult life, public library users are a smaller percentage of the population than in any other age group. It would appear that children's librarians must be doing something right, and that young adult and adult librarians need to do a better job than they are now doing in serving the vital life interests of people.

Fourth, as has been stated by several speakers, children's library service today is in need of goals, objectives, planning and evaluation — in short, it is in need of a guiding theory. Goals are general ends, and by definition are never really achieved but can only be approximated. Objectives are more immediate and practical, and for best results they should: (1) be measurable, (2) relate to desired changes in the behavior of people, and (3) be realistic and practical. It is not difficult to establish measurable objectives (e.g., to serve all the children), but to phrase this objective in behavioral and measurable terms is difficult. We tend to say that the goal of children's library service is to contribute to the education of children, but we cannot specify just how this is done or with what particular behavioral changes in view. If we could identify such changes and measure them, we would then be able to ascertain (among other things) which of two or more alternate methods of accomplishing these changes is the more effective.

Practicality and realism in our objectives is necessary if we are not to be frustrated in our efforts to achieve the impossible. We need to take account of our resources in staff, money, materials, space and know-how, and to set our sights not far beyond those limits; available resources inevitably determine priorities. I doubt, for example, that we can really expect to serve all the children in our society, or to work with them on a one-to-one intensive basis. No field of public library service is much better off in this regard, in my opinion, and the general thrust of research seems to indicate that the public library is *not* a purposive educational influence.

But there are some ways open by which to grapple with this difficult and vexing problem. For example, there is the CIPP (Context, Input,

Product and Process) model, developed at Ohio State University and currently being required by the U.S. Office of Education of all state library agencies in preparing their 5-year plans under LSCA. Briefly, CIPP forces one to consider the main groups of variables which affect planning, and to spell out in detail general goals, objectives and specific activities on a year-to-year basis for achieving those objectives.

Notice that this general principle is summed up as indicating a need for theory. Theory is conspicuous by its absence in children's work (and to a large degree in all public library work). A theory is a general statement of major relationships known or thought to be true about the phenomena constituting a given field of study. As such it can be intensely practical; it is often said that we lack a philosophy of librarianship, but I think that what is really meant is that we lack a guiding theory. To evolve such a theory is difficult but not impossible, and one practical suggestion is to borrow theory from other disciplines or other areas of librarianship. Information science has a well-developed body of theory, for example, and some of the institute speakers have emphasized that public libraries should serve the information needs of children. Information science has come to recognize a hierarchy of needs, beginning with a person's real or latent need, which may not completely match the expressed need, which in turn is often modified in becoming the need as understood by the librarian, and which again is constrained by available resources in the final state of the satisfied need. Children's librarians will find many more doors opening before them when they can express a well-developed theory of what they are doing and seek to do.

Fifth, public library services to children need periodically to be examined critically, to be adapted to new and changing circumstances, and to be evaluated; and new services should be tried out regularly, in an experimental mode. Children's librarians have developed new services, of course (e.g., dial-a-story, pajamas story hours, and toy-lending service), which is commendable and indicates the vitality of the field. But more insightful services are needed, e.g., getting mothers in inner-city culturally deprived families to read books regularly to their preschool children in order to improve their reading readiness.

Activity programs for children in particular seem not to be well thought out or logically sound. As has been stated earlier, Fasick and England in their recent survey of children's work in the Regina Public Library report that 80 percent of the children use the library in order to get books, and many fewer than that to attend programs. Pauline Wilson, in her recent book *A Communications Elite and the Public Library*, presents an analysis of adult programs which may be equally valid in regard to children's work. She sees two main functions or values of programs, viz., to stimulate use of the collection, and to serve as public relations devices. If this is so, then programs should be planned, conducted and evaluated for these ends and not for other (and usually more ambitious) ends.

Even standard or traditional services to children should not be exempt from scrutiny. I have never seen a study of reference service to children, but more than one-half dozen studies in recent years of public library adult reference service are agreed on one major point, viz., that about one-half the questions are answered incorrectly. If this is true of reference service to children, it is obviously imperative to correct the situation before the service is further publicized or expanded. We can all agree on the great need for improved measures of performance of library services, and this is particularly true of children's services.

Mention was made of the desirability of evolving (or at least testing) new services by means of experiments. Formal experiments require control groups and the comparison of data before and after the introduction of the experimental variable. Libraries are continually experimenting in an informal way, with the result that we are never quite sure how much of a change occurred or what caused it. Good experiments are not difficult to design, and we have had some good ones in librarianship already. As long ago as 1940, Lowell Martin planned a series of experiments in the South Chicago Branch Public Library. Adult fiction was to be identified by an innocuous symbol indicating each of several quality levels, and all patrons were to have identification numbers coded to indicate sex, age, education, and occupation. All books in the lowest-quality level of fiction were to be removed from the shelves, to see whether people who typically borrowed only those books would move up to the next higher level or leave the library. Unfortunately, Pearl Harbor forced cancellation of all these plans, and we still have no evidence as to whether or not providing comics or popular fiction series will lead children to anything else. It might be noted that experiments are best planned in the light of a guiding theory.

Sixth, the status and image of the children's librarian depends more on how they spend their time and what tasks they perform (and do not perform) than on any other factors. Some of the earlier papers give impressive lists of qualities desired of children's librarians, and one can hardly oppose or reject any of them. However, on one hand those attributes are desirable in all librarians and indeed in all people; on the other hand, few persons have even most of those traits. Furthermore, possession of personality traits or personal qualities is not the decisive factor separating high-status occupations from low. What counts is performance on the job.

The basic economic fact of modern life is that the American worker has increased his/her productivity at about 2 percent a year over the last fifty years, and this is what justifies increased real wages. To be sure, much of this increased productivity results from the use of more sophisticated equipment. Libraries now are beginning to use computers, for example, in cataloging and in circulation work, and already there are reports of increased productivity per hour of work. Use of complex equipment is not the only way to increase productivity; two other ways are to eliminate unnecessary work and to shift lower-level duties to less-qualified and lower-paid staff. Libraries have made great strides in simplifying borrower registration and in eliminating the slipping of books returned by patrons, but much still remains which could be questioned.

Shifting duties to lower-paid persons with less training is sometimes resisted by professional librarians. Increasingly, however, it is the hall-mark of the advanced professions, with the concomitant result that the people with the more advanced training are pushing back the frontiers of their work and doing tasks which no other group could possibly handle. Nurses today are performing many duties which ten or twenty years ago were performed by doctors, and doctors are doing heart transplants and other surgery previously deemed impossible. Dentists regularly used to clean the teeth of their patients; now dental hygienists do this just about as well as dentists could, while dentists use their time more for fillings and extractions. We librarians cannot keep any level of task for ourselves alone; on the contrary, we should insist on training others to perform the lowest level of what is commonly done by librarians, so that we are able to go on to the more difficult and more important tasks.

In most research libraries today it costs more to catalog a book than to buy it. In most cases, it costs almost as much to borrow a book by interlibrary loan as to buy it. Desirable though it may be to interloan children's books, the cost to society of doing so must be reckoned with. It seems to me that over the years, children's librarians have made particularly little change in the way they do their work, or in who performs which tasks. Most of us like to work with patrons; notice that many of the tasks transferred to less-qualified personnel in other professions are those which concern and involve the people served. This is part of the price of professionalism.

My seventh point is that children's librarians have had (and should have) a major concern for the size, composition and quality of the library's collection of materials for children. It may well be that this is the major service which librarians can perform for children: to assemble a large collection of representative materials, to organize them so that they are easy to find and to use, to provide a comfortable and attractive milieu, to inform children of their availability, and then to stay out of their way. It is symptomatic of children's work in today's world that this responsibility for materials is being steadily broadened, e.g., to secure access for children to adult books when appropriate and to juvenile materials in other libraries, and to fight for the rights of children to have intellectual freedom. The spirited discussions here this week on some of these points indicates that this responsibility is taken seriously. In general, it seems to me that children's librarians have long demonstrated great competence in this area.

Eighth, children's librarians need to acquire a lot of basic facts about their own work. By this I do not mean the sort of research about which Kingsbury writes, but rather a knowledge of many specific situations of any fairly recent date, from a good sample of public libraries across the country. Several questions were raised in this institute concerning practices in children's work, about which there is apparently no general knowledge, e.g., the number of public libraries which allow children to have access to adult books. I have been struck by the paucity of hard data in regard to children's work. People give their opinions and tell of their own experiences; these are the next best thing to evidence in the sense of verifiable observations, but not nearly as good. The 1974 U.S. Office of Education form for the national collection of public library data consisted of fifty-three questions, not one of which dealt with children's work. In a recent study of 49 state and provincial library agencies' published compilations of public library statistics, 1111 items in all were identified; of those, only 23 (2 percent) involved aspects of children's work (viz., number of children's books and number of juvenile loans).

This sort of applied or survey research can be done as well or better by individual librarians, and by library association members or committees, as by library school faculty or doctoral students. At the next higher level of complexity, children's librarians would do well to replicate all appropriate studies of adult work, e.g., the analysis of the accuracy of librarians' answers to children's reference questions. No one can do this as well or with as much insight as the people who are daily engaged in the work in question.

The ninth and final generalization is that children's librarians are first of all public librarians and are not that special or different when compared to other professional librarians in public libraries. Some children's librarians seem to think of themselves as completely different from all other librarians, almost unique and unusual. But to judge from the remarks in these earlier papers (and from my own observations), you are concerned with service to adults as well as to children, and with adult literature as well as children's literature. Catalogers, adult reference librarians, and even public library directors all focus more on some tasks than on others, as do children's librarians, but all (including children's librarians) overlap and intersect with each other.

From a functional point of view, the problems of supervision and administration are much the same for all groups, as are those of planning and evaluation. All librarians need to be concerned with public relations, and with the political scene in the broad sense. Children's librarians are and will be necessarily involved in the general problems of public libraries (e.g., the difficulties of getting service to people in rural areas); they ought also to involve themselves in the projected solutions. Public libraries will be much the worse off for poorly developed children's departments, and children's librarians cannot expect to succeed while public libraries in general fail to prosper. With a distinguished past behind them, children's librarians can look forward to at least as great a future.

ACRONYMS

AASL — American Association of School Librarians
AFDC — Aid to Families with Dependent Children
ALA — American Library Association
ALSC — Association for Library Service to Children
ASLA — Association of State Library Agencies
BCPL — Baltimore County Public Library
CETA — Comprehensive Employment and Training Act
CIPP — Context, Input, Product and Process
DRA — Directed Reading Activity
DR-TA — Directed Reading-Thinking Activity
EPIE — Educational Products Information Exchange
ERIC — Educational Resources Information Center
ESEA — Elementary and Secondary Education Act
ITA — Initial Teaching Alphabet
LSCA — Library Services and Construction Act
MLS — Master's of Library Science
NCLIS — National Commission on Libraries and Information Science
PLA — Public Library Association
PS — Public School
PTA — Parent-Teacher Association
PUC — Pennsylvania Union Catalog
TOT — Time on Task
YASD — Young Adult Services Division
ZPG — Zero Population Growth

INDEX

Prepared by: Mary Kelly Black